T0118734

SUBSIDIA BIBLICA

5

The Message of the New Testament
and
the Aramaic Bible (Targum)

ROMAE
E PONTIFICIO INSTITUTO BIBLICO
1982

R. LE DÉAUT

The Message of the New Testament
and
the Aramaic Bible (Targum)

(Revised edition of *Liturgie juive et Nouveau Testament,* 1965)

Translated from the French
by
STEPHEN F. MILETIC

ROME
BIBLICAL INSTITUTE PRESS
1982

This is a translation and revision of R. Le Déaut, *Liturgie juive et Nouveau Testament*. Rome 1965. Pontifical Biblical Institute. Revision by the author. Translation by Stephen F. Miletic in collaboration with the author.

© Iura editionis et versionis reservantur
PRINTED IN ITALY

TYPIS P. U. G. - ROMAE — COMPOSITIO IBM
IMPRESSIO OFFSET

Cordially dedicated to my former students at Duquesne University (Pittsburgh) and Tulane University (New Orleans).

Preface

Twenty years ago who would have thought it possible that the term *targum* would become almost a familiar one to students in schools of theology? A majority now know that *targum* is a Hebrew word which means "translation" and that targums are ancient versions of the Bible in the Aramaic language. In the synagogue, after each verse was read from the Hebrew Pentateuch, a translator (called *meturgeman*) would recite by heart the Aramaic translation. With respect to the Prophets, he would comment on each group of three verses. These data form part of the body of knowledge which confronts the average student of today. Perhaps a few students have even read some targumic texts (or at least heard them read aloud by their professors). All of this has become possible since editions and translations have multiplied in the last few years.

Targumic studies have, in fact, encountered a surprising renewal of interest. This is due, to a large extent, to the discovery of important texts such as the targums of *Job* and *Leviticus* at Qumran. Other important discoveries include the complete targumic text of the Pentateuch (*Codex Neofiti* 1, in the Vatican Library). One expert, W. D. Davies, notes with some satisfaction: "Most recently there has been a salutary return to the study of the Targumim in relation to the NT" (*Paul and Rabbinic Judaism*, Revised Edition, New York, 1967, p. xv).

In 1965 I published a short book (*Liturgie juive et Nouveau Testament: Le témoignage des versions araméennes*), for which it was suggested that I prepare an English edition and that such an English edition would provide students in North America and elsewhere with an introduction to targumic literature. This short study was a development from a lecture given to non-specialists at the Biblical Institute in Rome on January 17, 1965.

My goal was to demonstrate how ancient Jewish liturgy and the Aramaic translations connected with it constitute a capital source for illustrating the message of the New Testament. Examples were given to show the interest of this source and to illustrate a method of research for comparing targumic traditions and Christian texts. There was no time for long developments and technical discussions: the bibliography gave references to specialized works for later study. Rather, this more general presentation sought simply to bring attention to the neglected riches which are common to both the Synagogue and the Church.

Since that time targumic research has made considerable progress. Thus it has been necessary to update a number of points, to nuance and even modify certain affirmations so as to remain abreast of the current state of targumic studies. The notes and bibliography have also been revised from this perspective. They offer the student the possibility of pursuing certain interests and questions further.

So as to keep the book on the level of popularization, I have resisted the temptation of multiplying and expanding the footnotes. And this was done in spite of the recent and exciting developments in the area. At the first reading, the student is invited to read the text straight through, without looking at the notes on every occasion. Then later, when there is more leisure time, the reader could return to the problems which have aroused his or her curiosity.

At first, some readers might experience a certain uncomfortableness in entering a world of thought so foreign to the one they are used to, and in discovering a use of the Bible so different from our modern concepts of scriptural exegesis. Yet who could ignore the value of discovering as exactly as possible the manner in which the Bible was interpreted in the very milieu in which Jesus and his first disciples lived?

Once an interest and sympathy has been aroused for this patrimony common to Israel and the Church, which goes back to the Jewish dawn of Christian faith, it will then be seen that many problems and aspects which once seemed purely "archeological" now confront us, too, as we try to understand what the Word of God is saying to us today, and to "translate" this for our contemporaries.

Roger Le Déaut, C.S.Sp.

Rome, April 19, 1981
(A day on which both Jews and Christians happened to celebrate Passover)

Translator's Note

The translator would like to acknowledge the gracious assistance of the Diocese of London, Ontario Canada, furnished by the Most Reverend John Michael Sherlock, Bishop. The undersigned would also like to acknowledge his debt to Dr. R. Mitchell, Fr. J. Zeitz and Dr. B. Coste.

Finally, it remains to thank Fr. R. Le Déaut for his kindness and encouragement throughout this project. His combined talents as teacher-scholar are demonstrated in this book by his ability to introduce the neophyte to a complex subject matter. It is the hope of the translator that his work has not encumbered but enhanced the dialogue between scholar and novice.

September, 1981

Stephen F. Miletic
Marquette University
Milwaukee, Wisconsin

Table of Contents

Abbreviations

Billerbeck	H. L. Strack and P. Billerbeck, *Kommentar zum neuen Testament aus Talmud und Midrasch* (6 vols; Munich, 1922-1961)
BZ	*Biblische Zeitschrift*
CBQ	*Catholic Biblical Quarterly*
DBS	*Supplément au Dictionnaire de la Bible* (Paris)
HTR	*Harvard Theological Review*
HUCA	*Hebrew Union College Annual*
JBL	*Journal of Biblical Literature*
JJS	*Journal of Jewish Studies*
JQR	*Jewish Quarterly Review*
JSJ	*Journal for the Study of Judaism*
Judaism	G. F. Moore, *Judaism in the First Centuries of the Christian Era*, (3 vols.; Cambridge, Mass. 1932)
LXX	Septuagint
NTS	*New Testament Studies*
PL	*Patrologia latina* (J. Migne, Paris)
RB	*Revue biblique*
REJ	*Revue des Etudes juives*
RSPT	*Revue des Sciences philosophiques et théologiques*
RSR	*Recherches de Science religieuse*
SC	*Sources chrétiennes* (Paris)
TS	*Theological Studies*
TZ	*Theologische Zeitschrift*
ZNW	*Zeitschrift für die neutestamentliche Wissenschaft*

Introduction

Ever since the distant days when critical method became a tool of exegesis, the necessity for precise knowledge concerning the historical, social, religious and cultural background in which Christianity developed has been acknowledged. History, archaeology, the comparative study of religions and civilizations have permitted us to situate the milieu of the Bible in a broader framework. Now we do not examine the Bible as if it were "in isolation, paying attention only to the text as it has been transmitted" (R. de Vaux). More precisely, we have learnt to better determine the literary and doctrinal milieu in which the sacred books developed. We have especially studied the Jewish traditions contemporaneous with the beginning of our era, and this knowledge is now considered by all to be irreplacable for anyone who would understand the writings of the New Testament. This background includes the worlds of Apocryphal and Apocalyptic literature, of Hellenism, of ancient Jewish sects such as the Essenes (who for forty years have held our attention because of the discovery of the manuscripts in the Judaean desert). In a number of the above-mentioned writings, one recognizes some relationship to Christianity. But in the case of Apocryphal literature we are often in the presence of works that have been manipulated and reworked by Christian hands. We need only mention the controversies concerning the true nature and origins of the *Testaments of the XII Patriarchs* and the *Odes of Solomon*. In the case of Hellenism and Qumran, proof of a true dependence must be demonstrated in each instance.

Above all else, the problem is to determine as completely and precisely as possible the authentic background of the writings in question. The general use of the comparative method has produced too many new approaches which have led to impasses. As a result, we cannot accept without a severe critique all the affinities discovered within the currents of thought dominant in the Near East of the first century.

Now there is certainly a common ground between Christianity and the religion of the Old Testament: that of the Bible. But how did the Bible (i.e., the Old Testament) find its way into the New Testament?

Scripture and Tradition

We are in the habit of thinking that the sacred text of the Old Testament came into the hands of the Christians in about the same form as our modern-day text. We also think that the Christians, following the example of their Master, reinterpreted it and "completed" it with the teachings and history of Jesus and his first disciples. However, did the Bible come down to them totally alone or did it have a long-standing interpretative tradition already accompanying it? R. Bloch has addressed this question in the title of one of her articles, a title that was taken up again in a very fine book by G. Vermes, *Ecriture et Tradition dans le Judaïsme*[1]. An examination of the connections between Scripture and Tradition in Jewish thought would show that this is a fundamental question and that its solution would be valuable and relevant in recent discussions within the Catholic Church (even regarding the nature of the inspiration of Scripture). In effect, it is absolutely certain that the two were not separated and that the sacred text was not considered independently from its traditional interpretation. It is to be noted, for example, that the latter has always tended to enter into the text itself of the ancient translations which thus become precious witnesses of the evolution of religious ideas. We shall see a number of examples of this in what follows. Scripture and Tradition formed one unique source of revelation which was continually evolving under the guidance of the Spirit.

Even within the Old Testament, did not the most creative among the Prophets remain attached to a tradition which they used

---

[1] *Cahiers Sioniens*, 1 (1954) pp. 9-34. G. Vermes, *Scripture and Tradition in Judaism*, Leiden, 1961 (reprinted in 1973). See also the second edition of L. Bouyer's, *La Bible et L'Evangile*, Paris, 1958 (ET: *The Meaning of Sacred Scripture*. Translated by M. P. Ryan, Notre Dame, 1958).

and developed? For example, "Isaiah develops material from Amos; Jeremiah manifests influences from Hosea and Isaiah; Ezekiel, beyond his relationship to the Holiness Code, makes use of Amos, Hosea, Isaiah and especially Jeremiah" (R. Bloch, *DBS*, V, p. 1270)[2]. Revelation was addressed to a living people, the people of God, who guarded the Word which they had to transmit faithfully (*Psalm* 78. 1-8) and which cannot be separated from concrete historical experience. Does not Isaiah call Israel "the people in whose heart is my Torah" (*Isaiah* 51.7)[3]? The coming of the Messiah was not preceded by any bookish preparation, but by a progressive education of the soul for the reception of the Gospel message.

We should also remember the evident fact that, given the scarcity of copies of the Bible, very few people (those who knew how to read and those fortunate to own a copy)[4] could know exactly what was Word of God contained in the holy books and what was a gloss or exegesis. This Word reached the faithful by hearing (*fides ex auditu*, "faith from hearing", as it were) in the school classes but more especially in synagogue preaching. In Jewish terminology oral tradition is called *Torah* (*Shabbath* 31 a), but more precisely *Torah she be-'al peh* ("oral teaching"). Its authority was not less than the authority of the written Torah. All the biblical books of the Jewish canon outside of the Pentateuch are classified by the Talmud among the *dibrē qabbalah* or "words of the Tradition".[5]

If the discovery at Qumran of a complete manuscript of Isaiah prior to our era is an exciting scientific event, from another perspective it is equally important to know how the reader of the first

---

[2] B. Renaud, in his *Structure et attaches littéraires de Michée IV-V*, Paris, 1964, has shown that chapters four and five constitute "a kind of midrash, that is to say, a commentary and an actualization of ancient texts" (A.-M. Dubarle, *RSPT* 49 [1965] p. 475) to respond to Israel's situation in the fifth century before our era.

[3] This passage is marked by a sign in the Qumran manuscript of Isaiah. See G. R. Driver, *The Judaean Scrolls*, Oxford, 1965, p. 528.

[4] On the rarity of the manuscripts and the extreme care in handling them see *B.M.* 29b. Already Jerome (PL 22,746) complained about the extravagant price paid for Origen's works: "Nostrum marsupium alexandrinae chartae evacuarunt" ("The Alexandrian papers [papyri] have emptied our purse").

[5] See R. Bloch, *art. cit.*, p. 11; W. Bacher, *Die exegetische Terminologie der jüdischen Traditionsliteratur*, Leipzig, 1899, pp. 155, 165.

century understood this text. Granted that the literal sense of the
Old Testament preserves its primordial value as revelation, in the
study of the transition to the new religion which issues forth from
the Book it is important to see the meaning these texts had when
they served as relays or links in a living and harmonious continuum.
One must constantly keep in mind that the authors of the New
Testament were Jews nourished by their very own tradition and
milieu, speaking and writing mainly for other Jews of the same
tradition. They were not faced with a Bible that was "chemically
pure" of all later infiltration, the kind recent modern exegetes have
postulated as the necessary point of departure for their research.

Tradition and Liturgy

How was this tradition developed? Throughout the history of
the chosen people there existed an oral tradition independent of
Scripture but more and more of which was progressively committed
to writing. Here I am only speaking about the oral tradition which
was born from explanation of the Scriptures, which leads me to
speak about the essential role of biblical translations.

Immediate familiarity with the strange word *Targum* is probably best attained by the realization that it simply means "translation". Without being directly aware of it we have all used "targums"
when reading our favorite authors who originally wrote in foreign
languages: Dostoyevsky, Pushkin, Bergson, Sartre, according to one's
taste! The Greek translation known as the Septuagint (LXX) is
also a targum. But in a stricter sense this term refers to translations
of the Hebrew text of the Old Testament into the Aramaic language,
for use in the synagogue.

Early in Israel's history, Hebrew was the common language of
the Jews, as is indicated in *2 Kings* 18.26 (701 B.C.). After the
exile (587 B.C.), the large majority of the people slowly adopted
the international language of that time: Aramaic. Eventually they
were not able to understand the biblical text (which was in Hebrew)
without a translation and commentary. Certain scholars, in agreement with the Jewish tradition (*Meg.* 3a), see the first appearance of
Aramaic translations in *Nehemiah* (8.8):

> (Ezra) read from the book, from the law of God, *translating
> and giving the sense*, so that the people understood the read-
> ing.

It was considered inconceivable that a reading for a general audience from the Word of God be only from the Hebrew: it would have been unintelligible to them.[6] So the practice started of translating the text which was read within the liturgical assemblies, just as we Latin-rite Catholics used to translate the epistles and gospels of our Latin masses. At first, targumic tradition was oral, and even in later centuries, according to Rabbinic literature, the targums were to be recited in the synagogue without the help of a written text. The discovery of targumic fragments from the book of *Job* and from *Leviticus* in caves 4 and 11 at Qumran confirms the existence of Aramaic translations of biblical books before the time of Christ.[7]

Here we must insist on the importance of the milieu in which the translations of the Old Testament were elaborated: the Jewish liturgy. The dependence of the Christian liturgy on Jewish liturgy has long been recognized. Recent studies have more and more demonstrated how profound and vast this influence was, especially in those churches which, in terms of language and tradition, have remained close to their Jewish inheritance (as with the Syrian churches).[8] A. Baumstark has studied a number of these influences and has synthetized this research in his *Liturgie comparée*.[9] We need merely recall the influence of the Jewish Passover Haggadah and the Jewish benedictions on Christian Eucharist prayers; or the formation of the liturgy of the Hours (whose essence is still the Psalms of Israel); or the institution of fasting, etc. D. Flusser, professor at the

---

[6] For the wording of *Nehemiah* 8.8 see M. McNamara, *Targum and Testament*, Grand Rapids, Mich., 1972, pp. 22-23 and 79-81. Note especially verse 12 "And all the people went their way to eat and drink... *because they* had *understood* the words that were declared to them".

[7] J. P. M. van der Ploeg – A. S. van der Woude, *Le Targum de Job de la grotte XI de Qumrân*, Leiden, 1971; M. Sokoloff, *The Targum to Job from Qumran Cave XI*, Ramat-Gan, 1974; J. T. Milik, *Qumrân grotte 4*, II (Discoveries in the Judaean Desert VI), II. *Tefillin, Mezuzot et Targums* (4Q128 - 4Q157), Oxford, 1977. The above reference confirms the intuition of the scholar L. Zunz: "During the period of the Hasmoneans, there certainly already existed *written* Aramaic translations for most of the biblical books" (*Die gottesdienstlichen Vorträge der Juden*[2], Frankfurt A.M., 1892, p. 65).

[8] See K. Hruby, *L'Orient syrien* 9 (1964) p. 512.

[9] See the third edition, revised by B. Botte, Chevetogne, 1953. (ET: *Comparative Liturgy*. Translated by F. L. Cross, London, 1958). Note that this book is often cited by J. Heinemann, *Prayer in the Talmud: Form and Patterns*, Berlin/New York, 1977.

Hebrew University of Jerusalem, has shown the connections of the
Sanctus and the *Gloria* with the ancient Jewish prayer of the *Qedushah*.[10]   As might be expected, this particular dependence most
often is discernible only when we take into account the intermediary
biblical translations and Jewish exegesis. The tripartite division of
the *Gloria in excelsis Deo* is confirmed by the targumic commentary
on the triple "Holy" of *Isaiah* 6.3:

> The Holiness of God appears:
> In the highest, as *Glory*
> on earth, as *Peace*
> for men, as (God's) *Good Pleasure*.[11]

Two apparently contradictory aspects of any liturgy have often
been pointed out. Liturgy is a living institution, yet at the same
time essentially traditional, conservative. In Israel, it was the mani-
festation of the spiritual life of the people of God. In the absence of
any systematic theology, the Scriptures and their commentaries
summed up the religion of the community. Especially after the
exile, it was always by means of the ancient Scriptures that the
problems of the present were solved (the prophetic flame being dead,
cf. *Psalm* 74.9). This meditation of Scripture (*midrash*) would then
itself become the source of new writings, whose study would engen-
der still other traditions. The influence of the liturgical environment
on the development of the Old Testament writings is admitted by all
exegetes, who differ only on the extent of this influence.

On the other hand, liturgy is essentially conservative.[12] This
aspect of liturgy is well confirmed by the spontaneous reactions of
Latin-rite Catholics to the recent reforms, even when it was simply a

---

[10] "Sanktus und Gloria" in *Abraham unser Vater* (Festschrift für O. Mi-
chel), Leiden, 1963, pp. 129-152. The mutual dependence of the two liturgies
is so evident to him that he writes: "Can we actually imagine that a Christian
would have dared change one word of the Old Testament without relying for
that on some Jewish liturgical tradition?" (p. 131).

[11] See W. O. E. Oesterley, *The Jewish Background of the Christian Liturgy*,
Oxford, 1925. One can find a significant example in A. Cabaniss, "A Jewish
Provenience of the Advent Antiphons", *JQR* 66 (1975-1976) pp. 39-56. On
page 39 he writes, "It is no secret that Christian liturgy is indebted in numerous
ways to Jewish sources".

[12] "The Haggadah is a piece of liturgy, and it is more difficult to expurgate
liturgy than almost any other kind of literature" (D. Daube, *The New Testament
and Rabbinic Judaism*, London, 1956 [reprinted 1973], p. 9).

matter of displacing a comma in the *Preface* (Domine, *sancte Pater*, omnipotens: "Lord, Holy Father, almighty")! This characteristic, which in itself can be problematic, nevertheless has an advantage for us since we can return by means of the liturgy to a far distant period. Several Jewish scholars think, for example, that the ritual of the Passover preserves texts which clearly predate the Christian era.[13] One does not easily change the rites and texts which, throughout centuries, have expressed the piety of a people. For a long time some passages were preserved in the Roman liturgy which are clearly corrupt in the manuscript tradition. One example can be found in the former rite of baptism. Here there was a mistake caused by "betacism" (the confusing of "b" for "v"): *appropinquabit enim judicium Dei* ("For the judgment of God will draw near") instead of *appropinquavit* ("has drawn near"). This conservative thrust explains how the Jewish people would have preserved and utilized texts within the synagogue which were not in line with the legislation of the *Mishnah* (which was compiled around A.D. 200). It also explains how in Palestine, even after the arrival in the tenth century of the Babylonian Targum (the so-called *Onkelos* – a rather literal translation), the ancient Palestinian Targum with its more delightful paraphrases continued to be read at the great feasts. This fact was undoubtedly responsible for its not having completely disappeared. On those days, the Jewish worshippers could not resist listening to beautiful haggadic commentaries, just as for many believers, until recently, there could be no real Christmas in France without the hymn *Minuit chrétiens*, or in Germany without the hymn *Stille Nacht*. The antiquity of certain parts of the Palestinian Targum also comes from the fact that the *haggadah* (traditions based on homiletic commentaries of Scripture) is more stable than the *halakhah* (commentaries of a juridical or moral nature, giving norms of conduct) which by definition has to be continually adapted. In the case of *haggadah*, on the other hand, the traditional explanations were cherished and jealously preserved, though occasionaly some new gem was added. In understanding Christian interpretation of the Old Testament in light of Jewish tradition, it is the liturgical *haggadah* which represents the most interesting source, since continuity is

---

[13] So L. Finkelstein, "Pre-Maccabean Documents in the Passover Haggadah", *HTR* 35 (1942) pp. 291-332; 36 (1943) pp. 1-39; for the *Qedushah*, see D. Flusser, *art. cit.*, pp. 143-144.

more certain than with the *halakhah* whose only relationship to the Christian tradition is often one of rupture.

Jewish Liturgy and the New Testament

The New Testament clearly affirms this fact: the Christian message first resounded in the villages of Palestine and of the Jewish Diaspora, within local synagogues and in the meeting places of liturgical assemblies. Jesus himself spoke in the synagogues; once at least, in Nazareth, his preaching of the Good News is connected explicitly to the prior reading from the prophet Isaiah (*Luke* 4.16-28). The discourse on the Bread of Life in the synagogue of Capernaum (see *John* 6.59) could have been based on the texts of the Law and the Prophets just read.[14] Just as Christ himself, Paul first and foremost sought to show the Jewish people how the sacred history of Israel continued in Jesus (*Acts* 9.20: Damascus; 13.16: Antioch in Pisidia; 14.1: Iconium; 17.1-4: Thessalonica; 18.4-8: Corinth; 28.23-28: Rome). One can easily imagine how the role of the translator-commentator (which will be codified in *Mishnah Meg.* IV) was of great occasion for those preachers eager to spread their doctrines. This role provided the Christians a privileged moment to reveal the profound meaning of the Scriptures in light of their fulfillment. Since Jews and Christians had the same Bible in common, only the interpretations given to it by one and the other created a distinction and founded a different faith.

Since the *meturgeman* was usually a cultured person it is probable that through him certain ideas central to Apocalypticism (or Hellenism) were spread in the Jewish world. The Essenes (who were especially consecrated to the study of the Law) probably spread their ideas throughout the villages of Palestine (as did Jesus). Their asceticism, their messianic expectations, their alienation from the Temple cult, etc. — all of this would have paved the way for the

---

[14] A. Guilding, *The Fourth Gospel and Jewish Worship*, Oxford, 1960, pp. 58-68. See the criticisms of L. Morris, *The New Testament and the Jewish Lectionaries*, London 1964; B. Gärtner, *John 6 and the Jewish Passover*, Lund 1959; P. Borgen, "Observations on the Midrashic Character of John 6", *ZNW* 54 (1963) pp. 232-240.

Gospel.[15]   Is there not here a possible explanation for the many characteristics common to both the writings from the Dead Sea and primitive Christianity?   In effect, it seems that, despite certain examples of intolerance that are understandable, a great deal of freedom for explanation was given preachers in the synagogues. The example of Paul is significant in this regard.

The role of ancient Jewish liturgy on the formation of the New Testament writings cannot be overlooked, especially for the gospel of John.   Reference has already been made above to *John* 6.   The following chapter clearly draws its thematic inspiration from the feast of Tabernacles.   With respect to the structure of the narrative, D. Mollat is certainly justified in writing:

> The guideposts for this gospel are the Jewish liturgical feasts: three Passovers (2.13; 6.4; 11.55); one undetermined feast (5.1); the feast of Tabernacles (7.2); the feast of the Dedication (10.22). These feasts, it seems, represent essential articulations of the Johannine gospel.[16]

Any understanding of Christian feasts such as Easter and Pentecost would be very impoverished were these not situated within the rich framework of Jewish tradition where they were born.[17] The liturgy of the Temple and that of the synagogue (both of which were familiar to the first Christians) could, to a large extent, be considered as the cradle of the new religion.

---

[15] The Essenes were not confined to Qumran but were established "in large numbers in every town" (Josephus, *Jewish War* II, §124).   The oath they made to "report none of their secrets to others" (*Jewish War* §141) would not stop them from discreet proselytizing in the surrounding areas.

[16] The quotation is translated from the fascicle edition of the *Bible de Jérusalem*, Paris, 1955, p. 32.   In his "The Earliest Structure of the Gospels", (*NTS* 5 [1958-1959] pp. 174-187), D. Daube has underscored the influence of the passover Haggadah on the formation of the gospels (he calls it "the matrix of Gospel tradition", p. 187).   See also J. J. Petuchowski, "Do this in Remembrance of me", *JBL* 76 (1957) pp. 293-298; F. Gavin, "Rabbinic Parallels in Early Church Orders", *HUCA* 6 (1929) pp. 55-57 (reprinted in J. J. Petuchowski, *Contributions to the Scientific Study of Jewish Liturgy*, New York, 1970, pp. 305-317).

[17] See R. Le Déaut, *La nuit pascale* (Analecta Biblica 22), Rome, 1963, (second reprint 1980); J. Potin, *La fête juive de la Pentecôte*, Paris, 1971.   On Pentecost and *Acts* 2 see M. Weinfeld, "Pentecost as Festival of the Giving of the Law", *Immanuel* 8 (1978) pp. 7-18; R. LeDéaut, "Šavūaʻot och den kristna pingsten i NT", *Svensk Exegetisk Årsbok* 44 (1979) pp. 148-170.

The Character of the Biblical Translations

Targumic literature was born from reading the Scriptures and preaching within the synagogues, and many passages have preserved traces of the literary genre of homily: the use of the second person, the transition from the singular to the plural, direct interpellations, doxologies, and the frequent occurrence of "My people, my people, children of Israel...", introducing some prescript of the Law.[18] Except perhaps for the targums to the Writings, the targum cannot be considered nor understood independently of the community cult or the readings from the Law and Prophets which were commented on in the synagogue each Sabbath and feast day. From this translation and commentary develops the *midrash* which,

> ...designates a genre in which edification and explanation of the Scriptures are directly connected to the previous reading. Here the role of amplifying the text is real but secondary and is in the end always subordinate to its fundamental religious goal which is to emphasize the action of God, the Word of God.[19]

Situated within the immediate context of Scripture, the targum constitutes a link between the Bible and Jewish literature born from liturgical commentaries. Midrashic elaboration has been canonized many times by the sacred books themselves and should therefore be considered an important factor in the development of Revelation. It should also be taken into account in terms of understanding the growth of the inspired texts themselves upon which the doctrine of the New Testament will be built. Thus, for example, manna, which would quickly saturate the Israelites and be the cause of corrective punishment (*Numbers* 21.5), had become "nourishment of angels" (*Wisdom* 16.20), and the "bread of angels" in *Psalm* 78.25. The

---

[18] Here are some examples taken from varying recensions of the Palestinian targum: *Exodus* 20.2,3; 22.17; 23.2,19; 34.17,26; 35.3; *Leviticus* 19.11,26; 25. 37; *Numbers* 28.2; *Deuteronomy* 5.6,7,11; 6.16; 14.3,10. Even the arrangement of the Palestinian targum manuscripts reflects their homiletical use, see R. Bloch *REJ* 14 (1955) p. 7. Long ago L. Zunz brought to our attention the importance of liturgical commentaries for the development of midrash, *op. cit.*, pp. 75-76.

[19] R. Bloch, "Midrash", *DBS* V, p. 1263; cf. R. Le Déaut, "Apropos a Definition of Midrash", *Interpretation* 25 (1971) pp. 259-282.

story of the Exodus merely has *water* emerge from a rock while later *honey* will come forth (see *Psalm* 81.17; *Deuteronomy* 32.13). The importance of making reference to such ancient exegesis in order to understand Christian interpretation of the Old Testament is therefore apparent. Now this kind of exegesis is often preserved in the ancient translations, especially in the targums.

One of the reasons for the lack of interest in targumic sources in the past is that these texts were viewed as translations in the modern sense of the term: the faithful transferring of ideas from one language into another without adding or omitting anything. But if even a modern translator sometimes unconsciously gives excessive weight to a text, how could the ancient interpreters consider the Bible as a dead text, as a sacred mummy? To view a targumic source as a translation in the modern sense of the term is to ignore the ancient biblical conception of the living Word of God. The Word of God is living, addressed *hic et nunc* ("here and now") to human beings of all times. It maintains all of its practical value as the rule of life, from which flow religious teachings by constant adaptation to new situations. After all, this is the way the authors of the New Testament applied and adapted texts of the Old Testament (two significant examples of this are *Acts* 4.25-28 and *Hebrews* 3-4).

Since a text from the Law was followed by one from the Prophets, the commentator would often clarify one passage with the other because of the magnetism between the two pericopae. Thus, many targumic interpretations cannot be understood unless one recognizes allusions to another reading in the liturgy of that day.[20] One sees the advantage for New Testament exegesis of determining which biblical texts were read together in Palestinian

---

[20] C. Perrot has demonstrated how targumic commentaries betray such a reciprocal influence in the case of *Exodus* 21.1-22,23 and *Isaiah* 56.1-9, and how *Ephesians* 2.11-22 could have preserved traces of this complex background ("La lecture d'Exode XXI,1 - XXII,23 et son influence sur la littérature néo-testamentaire", in *A la rencontre de Dieu*, Mémorial A. Gelin, Le Puy, 1961, pp. 223-239). In W. Bacher, *Die Proömien der alten jüdischen Homilie* (Beihefte zur Zeitschrift für die alttestamentliche Wissenschaft 12), Leipzig, 1913, we find many examples which point out how the ancient Rabbis derived their support for their commentaries from several scriptural texts.

synagogues of the first century.[21]   It is certain that many New
Testament passages deploy the whole ensemble of scriptural argu-
mentation (from the Law and Prophets) which was developed by
Jewish teachers in the synagogue assemblies. The targums are
clearly quite different from translation in the conventional sense of
that word.

The primary goal of targumic translations is to make Scripture
understandable (see *Nehemiah* 8.8!). Even the supposedly literal
translation of Onkelos allows items to enter which one would fail to
find in the Hebrew original.[22]   This targum, which is based on the
ancient Palestinian targum (but was developed in Babylon) has
preserved many ancient interpretations in spite of the work of
editors and revisers.[23]

The homily presupposes exegesis because it was first necessary
to discover solutions to the enigmas within the text and answer
possible questions from the audience.   Even if we do not encounter
in the targum the classic phrase used by the Rabbis: "Why does the
Scripture say...?" (*mipeney mah*) when they were preparing to
analyze a passage, the solutions they sought are always there — ready,
acceptable, and often quite ingenious. Also, even the most discon-

---

[21] On the complicated problem of the lectionary cycles in the first centuries see J. Mann, *The Bible as Read and Preached in the Old Synagogue*, vol. I,
Cincinnati 1940 (reprinted New York, 1971, with an important prolegomenon
from B. Z. Wacholder); C. Perrot, *La lecture de la Bible dans la Synagogue —
Les anciennes lectures palestiniennes du Shabbat et des fêtes*, Hildesheim,
1973; J. Heinemann, "The Triennial Lectionary Cycle", *JJS* 19 (1968) pp. 41-
48; J. Reumann, "A History of Lectionaries", *Interpretation* 3 (1977) pp. 116-
138. Of the many interpretations of the New Testament in light of the lectionary cycles, we cite only M. D. Goulder, *Midrash and Lection in Matthew*,
London, 1974; *idem, The Evangelist's Calendar: A Lectionary Explanation of
the Development of Scripture*, London, 1978.

[22] A. Berliner, *Targum Onkelos*, Berlin, 1884, p. 206; G. Vermes, "Haggadah in the Onkelos Targum", *JSS* 8 (1963) pp. 159-169 (also printed in *Post-
Biblical Studies*, Leiden, 1975, pp. 127-138); J. W. Bowker, "Haggadah in the
Targum Onqelos", *JSS* 12 (1967) pp. 51-65. G. Vermes sums up the fundamental concern of ancient interpretations in this concise way: "[Onkelos]
renders the biblical text intelligible and theologically acceptable", *art. cit.*,
p. 169.

[23] In *Genesis* 17.17 Onkelos says that "Abraham fell on his face and
rejoiced". This is also the interpretation found in the *Book of Jubilees* 14.21;
15.17; compare *John* 8.56. Cf. R. Le Déaut, "Targumic Literature and New
Testament Interpretation", *Biblical Theology Bulletin* 4 (1974) p. 279.

certing passages (developed from originals which were certainly corrupt) are explained: I doubt if there is any place in all the targums where the commentator surrenders before a difficult text. How, indeed, could it be possible that an inspired text would have no meaning? Of course, the more complicated passages are those which reserve for us the best surprises. A few examples will illustrate the point. The present Hebrew text of 1 *Samuel* 13.1, when literally translated, reads: "Saul was one year old when he became king..." (this verse is replaced by three dots <...> and declared to be absurd by the *Jerusalem Bible*). The text actually means "Saul, when he began to reign was *like a one year old child* who has no sins" (Targum *ad loc*; cf. Symmachus).[24] The targum of *Deuteronomy* 1.2 explains why it took the Hebrews forty years to travel between Sinai and Palestine when, according to the biblical text, eleven days would have been sufficient: it was to punish them for their rebellion against YHWH that he made them wander for forty years. The problem of the incestuous marriages of the first descendants of Adam could not be avoided when reading *Leviticus* 20.17 which forbids marriage between brother and sister. By making good use of the double meaning of the Hebrew *ḥesed* ("shameful thing" or "favor"), the targum explains that this was a provisional toleration for the first humans before the promulgation of any law in the world (cf. *Romans* 7.9) so as to allow them to populate the universe. Why was Tamar condemned to being burnt alive (*Genesis* 38.24)? Quite simply because such is the punishment reserved for any daughter of a priest "who profanes herself by being a prostitute" (cf. *Leviticus* 21.9). The tradition had made Tamar a daughter of a priest (*Targum Genesis* 38.6, 24; *Baba Meṣia* 87 a), indeed Shem's own daughter (= Melchizedek) (see R. Meir in *Genesis Rabbah* on 38.24). And finally, there is nothing strange about the fact that the brothers of Joseph, because of his beard, did not recognize him (*Genesis* 42.8), because at the time he was sold to the Ishmaelites he was too young to have one! This list of examples could be extended, yet let us guard against labelling them as mere fantasy.

Here we can already see one characteristic particular to the Aramaic translations: their popular character. Here we are miles away from the scientific exegesis of Philo of Alexandria and much

---

[24] H. J. Schoeps, "Symmachus und der Midrasch", *Biblica* 28 (1948) pp. 34-35. See *Yoma* 22b. The Septuagint omits this verse.

closer to that of an Augustine making great efforts to bring to the
popolino ("the common people") of Hippo the mysteries of the
revealed word, and trying to capture their attention. So as to make
the text more lively, little anecdotes were added (which later developed into short novels in the midrashim), and I hesitate to believe
that some of them, because of their realism, were never told outside
of a limited audience. Does not the Mishnah prescribe that *Genesis*
35.22,[25] 2 *Samuel* 11.2-17 and 13.1-22 be left untranslated (*Meg.*
IV.10)?

The targumists love to dwell on the details of the text, and to
account for the most minute grammatical points. Thus, if the
Hebrew texts speaks of *stones* in *Genesis* 28.11 and of *one stone* in
v.18, it is because God, by a miracle, made them into a single one
(*T Genesis* 28.10). If *Genesis* 31.14 recalls that "Rachel and Leah
thus *responded*..." (the verb is singular in Hebrew), then this should
be understood as "Rachel *responded with the consent* of Leah..."
One finds names for anonymous places and people, a tendency which
has also been noted in the textual transmission of our gospels.[26]
Shem becomes Melchizedek, Balaam becomes Laban; Dinah, the
daughter of Jacob, becomes the wife of Job; David becomes the
cousin of Goliath; Balaam, Job and Jethro become the counselors
of Pharaoh; Hirah (*Genesis* 38.1) becomes King Hiram of Tyre;
Esdras is identified with Malachi (*Targum Mal.* 1,1; *Meg.* 15 a), etc.
For any sense of historical perspective is lacking in light of the principle formulated by the school of R. Ishmael: "There is no before
and after in Scripture"; i.e., the Bible does not necessarily follow a
chronological order. This disdain for chronology allowed one to
regroup texts useful for commentary and to bring in the history of

---

[25] Codex 440 of the Vatican Library (Fragmentary Targum) follows the
mishnaic prescription. It gives *Genesis* 35.22 in Hebrew and adds: "...not to
be translated." The *Book of Jubilees* (33.3) and the *Testament of Reuben*
(3.9-15), along with the most ancient Rabbis (*Shabbat* 55b), simply accept the
biblical tradition concerning the incest of Reuben while the targum of *Ps-Jonathan* attempts to acquit him.

[26] R. Le Déaut, *La nuit pascale*, pp. 59-60. The Sahidic translation and
the Bodmer Papyrus XIV (P[75]) give the name *Neues* to the evil rich man of
Luke 16. Cf. K. Grobel, "Whose Name was Neues", *NTS* 10 (1963-1964)
pp. 373-382. The apocryphal gospel of John will provide names not only for
the Samaritan woman but also for her parents and her five husbands (cf. G. Gal-
biati, *Mélanges E. Tisserant*, Città del Vaticano, vol. I, 1964, p. 211).

Israel persons of the distant past who had long since disappeared. It also explains how (in *Neofiti*) an allusion to Sarah's entry into Abimelech's harem can be placed on her lips in *Genesis* 16.5 even though this does not occur until *Genesis* 20.[27]

The tendency in popular tradition to name the anonymous will cause "the man who met Joseph wandering in the country" (*Genesis* 37.15) to be identified first as an angel, then as Gabriel in person. In the same way, one also notes that the servant of the high priest who had his ear cut off by Peter (Luke tells us it was the *right* ear) is, in the synoptic gospels, an anonymous figure, while in *John* 18.10 he has a name, Malchus.

The numerous historical applications of texts encountered in the targum contain a kind of beginning of typological interpretation: everything that has been written is relevant to the people of God (cf. *Romans* 15.14; *1 Corinthians* 10.1-12). There are even some interesting examples of double interpretations. On one level there is the literal meaning, and the second level is reserved for the people of Israel. Thus, in *Genesis* 40.12,18, Joseph gives two explanations of the dreams of the Pharaoh's officials. The first and more important applies to the future history of Israel (their own sojourn in Egypt, their oppression and deliverance), and is not in fact offered by Joseph for the benefit of the butler and the baker (it is even said that he is careful to keep it to himself) but for the congregation of the synagogue. The second interpretation directly concerns the baker and the butler, and follows the biblical account.

In this type of popular exegesis, one need not search very far for the reasons behind certain affirmations. The following, borrowed from a midrash, is quite clear and incontestable. If the plagues which the Egyptians suffered at the Red Sea were five times more severe than were the ones in Egypt, it is because the *hand* of God is being manifested (*Exodus* 14.31), and not just the *finger* of God (*Exodus* 8.19). One could find such subtleties naïve, but on the other hand, it would be wrong to forget what centuries of attentive scrutiny of the most minute points in Scripture have achieved by way of a deeper knowledge. Elements that had remained unnoticed suddenly, because of this indefatigable meditation, acquire a clear

---

[27] In *Sanhedrin* 101b, Cain asks God for forgiveness, in light of the forgiveness God will grant to the Israelites after the sin of the Golden Calf!

meaning in the presence of new circumstances.[28] And this can produce some real pearls, as in the translation of *Deuteronomy* 32.10:

> He (YHWH) watched over them and protected them, as the eyelid (*škn'*) protects the eye.[29]

In order to realize that the targums are not simple translations, it is sufficient to notice their great freedom in relation to the original Hebrew text, which they sometimes explain while deliberately turning their backs on the literal meaning.[30] This was done because of the excellent principle that the Bible must be explained by the *whole* Bible and by Tradition. This fact demonstrates that the ancients were not, without qualification, slaves to the letter, as is often claimed. We can also understand much better the freedom which Flavius Josephus took when rewriting sacred history while claiming to stay very close to his revealed sources:

> The precise details of our Scripture records will be set forth, each in its place, as my narrative proceeds, that being the procedure that I promised to follow throughout this work, neither adding nor omitting anything.
>
> (Thackeray's translation of *Jewish Antiquities* I, § 17.)

Even a superficial reading of his *Antiquities* shows that they are far from the kind of faithful transposition he promises. Pseudo-Philo, whose *Liber Antiquitatum Biblicarum* is a sort of biblical history from Adam to the death of Saul, offers the reader a large number of original developments based on sections of the Bible which, in his opinion, were too laconic. He even composes passages that are

---

[28] "...comme le bœuf qui rumine trouve dans l'herbe remâchée le goût de graines et de fleurs qu'il a broutées sans le savoir" ("...just as the cow which chews the cud finds within the herbage the taste of grain and flower which it first ate without knowing it", in M. Pagnol, *Le Château de ma mère*, pp. 105-106). Concerning tradition as the source of progress and of renewal within Judaism, see G. Scholem, "Tradition und Kommentar als religiöse Kategorien im Judentum", *Eranos Jahrbuch* 31 (1962) pp. 19-48.

[29] The quotation is from M. Black, *An Aramaic Approach to the Gospels and Acts*,[3] Oxford, 1973, p. 308. The paraphrase contains a play on the words *Shekinah* (Presence of God) and *šekina'* (eyelid).

[30] A list of well analyzed examples can be found in M. L. Klein, "Converse Translation: A Targumic Technique", *Biblica* 57 (1976) pp. 515-537.

quite different from those of the biblical authors (cf. c. 32: the canticle of Deborah). With an interest in the attitude towards the sacred text, it would be informative to study the later glosses, the *Qerē* ("Read") and the *Ketib* ("It is written") whose choices presuppose an interpretation. Especially interesting to study would be the *Tiqqunē sopherim* ("corrections of the scribes") whose retouching of the text reveals theological preoccupations.[31]

In any case, the attitude of the targumist is both one of fidelity to the "spirit" of the Scripture and of a certain independence from being too closely connected to the "letter".

Here are some significant examples in this regard. *Deuteronomy* 2.6 reads: "The food which you shall eat, you shall purchase.... Purchase their water, that you may drink...". In order to resolve clearly the difficulty of reconciling this verse with the tradition about manna and the well (or rock) which followed Israel in the desert (cf. *1 Corinthians* 10.4), this verse becomes:

> You do not need to buy food from them (the sons of Esau) for money, since manna descends for you from heaven; likewise you do not need to buy water from them, since the well of water ascends with you to the mountain tops and (descends) to the deep valleys.

One sees that within this conflict between Scripture and Tradition it is Tradition which wins out! In *Numbers* 12.1 the Hebrew text states twice that Moses had married a "Cushite woman" (*Aithiopissa* in the Greek). Yet it appeared shocking that the great prophet would choose a wife from another nation. Pseudo-Jonathan explains that while sojourning in Ethiopia, Moses was forced to marry the Queen, whom he of course repudiated afterwards.[32] The Onkelos targum (which here appears to summarize the Palestinian version) speaks prudently of a "beautiful" woman while the other targums say outrightly that "she was not a Cushite". This term signifies only that:

---

[31] See G. Vermes, *Scripture and Tradition in Judaism*, p. 228; D. Barthélemy, *Les Tiqquné sopherim et la critique textuelle de l'Ancien Testament*, *Suppl. to Vet. Test.*, vol. IX, Leiden, 1963, pp. 285-304.

[32] On the legend of Moses' sojourn in Ethiopia see G. Vermes in *Moïse, l'homme de l'Alliance*, Paris, 1955 (fascicles 2-3-4 of *Cahiers Sioniens*, 1954) p. 69.

as the Cushite is different in his body from every other
creature, so was Zipporah, the wife of Moses, handsome in
form and *beautiful in appearance* and distinguished in good
works more than all the women of that generation.[33]

In *Deuteronomy* 28.36,64 the prediction that when in exile
Israel "will serve other gods" is transformed to "You will pay taxes
to worshippers of idols." Likewise a completely different vision of
Israel's history is preserved in *Deuteronomy* 3.29. Here the Targum
mentions a collective repentance of the people at Peor (cf. *Numbers*
25.6):

> And we dwelt in the valley, weeping for our faults and
> confessing our sins, because we had been joined with the
> worshippers of the idols of Peor.

In *Genesis* 4.23b-24 we read: "*I have killed* a man because of a
wound, a child because of a bruise. For Cain is avenged seven times,
but Lamech seventy-seven times." The targum affirms the opposite
and interprets the passage as referring to the "forgiveness" given to
Lamech:

> If (for) Cain, who killed Abel, (judgement) has been suspend-
> ed for him for seven generations, for Lamech, *who did not
> kill*, it is just that (judgement) be suspended for him: for
> seventy-seven generations it will be suspended for him.

A. Díez Macho has noted that in replacing "seventy-seven generations" with "seventy-seven times" one finds a striking parallel to
Jesus' response to Peter who asks about the number of times he
should forgive his brother. "And Jesus said to him, 'I do not say
to you seven times, but seventy-seven times'" (*Matthew* 18.22).[34]
The gloss in the targum to *Genesis* 37.33, which contradicts the
Hebrew text, reads:

---

[33] The numerical value of *kushît* (736) is tantamount to *yephat mar'eh*
("beautiful in appearance"), see H. L. Strack, *Introduction to the Talmud*,
New York, 1969, pp. 97 and 295. There are other exegeses of *kushît* in *Mo'ed
Katan* 16b.

[34] "Targum y Nuevo Testamento", in *Mélanges E. Tisserant*, I, p. 182.
On the diverse recensions of the targum see M. L. Klein, "Converse Translation", p. 518; for the following example see his p. 522.

Neither a wild beast has devoured him, nor has he been killed by the hand of men: but I see, by the holy spirit, that a wicked woman (the wife of Potiphar) stands against him.

Thus, in order to introduce a more profound interpretation of Joseph's history into the commentary within the synagogue (which conforms to reality since it is known that Joseph is not dead), the meturgeman, without any scruples, reads the text with a meaning opposite to what is in the text. When *Genesis* 4.26 tells us: "He (Enosh) was the first to invoke the name of YHWH," we are surprised to see the Aramaic translation read into this text the beginning of idolatry:

Then the sons of man began to make themselves idols and to call them by the name of *Memra* (Word) of the Lord.[35]

These are only a few instances of the many possible ones which illustrate the freedom the translator exercised vis-à-vis the original Hebrew text. Besides, the translator had at his disposal certain traditional exegetical techniques which permitted him to surpass the obvious sense and discover new meanings which the modern exegete would never reach.

One of the most common techniques derives from the fact that Hebrew was written with only the consonants. Thus the interpreter could give to the consonants of many words in the text several possible vocalizations so as to extract all the possible meanings of the word. As a result, in *Genesis* 22.14 the word *shem* ("name") was read as *sham* ("there"), which explains the Onkelos text: "Abraham worshipped and prayed *there, in that place*." The very mention of Abraham's prayer could have arisen from the same Hebrew text, according to the method which unites or separates words in different ways and then interprets them. The Bible informs us that "Abraham called (verb *qara'*) the name of that place: "The Lord will provide." But *qara'* can also mean "to pray" and *shem* ("name") is an ancient substitute for YHWH. One could therefore read: "And

---

[35] See the commentary of J. Bowker, *The Targums and Rabbinic Literature*, Cambridge, 1969, p. 140 and P. Schäfer, "Der Götzendienst des Enosch", in *Studien zur Geschichte und Theologie des rabbinischen Judentums*, Leiden, 1978, pp. 134-152.

Abraham invoked the Name (i.e., God)..." In fact here the Palestinian targum has preserved a long prayer of Abraham in favor of Isaac's descendants.

In the same chapter (v. 8), this exegetical process has led to an interpretation whose theological importance has not been sufficiently perceived. Abraham replies to Isaac, who is worried about the sacrificial lamb: "It is God who will provide a lamb for the holocaust, my son." The targumists end up making Isaac the lamb for the holocaust by dividing the sentence in the following manner: "God sees to it; (with regard to) the lamb for the holocaust, (it is) my son". Thus they propose this translation (*Neofiti*):

> From before the Lord a lamb has been prepared (*'zdmn*); otherwise you are the lamb of the holocaust.[36]

In *Exodus* 15.2, from the formula "the God of my father", the vocative "my father" (*'abî*) has been isolated; so that, as a result, the targum (following the example of *Wisdom* 10.21, which associates the Hebrew children with the canticle of *Exodus* 15) has the children speaking as follows:[37]

> This is *our Father* who nourished us with honey from the rock and anointed us with oil from the flint stone.

This technique of interpretation was facilitated because of the absence of punctuation in ancient texts and of vocalization in the original Hebrew text. This technique was amply developed in Rabbinic exegesis, and whatever its scientific value it contributes to the development of Tradition and the creating of a treasure which has inspired Christian exegesis many times over.

These methods, of course, are not restricted to Aramaic translations. Even the Septuagint, while generally closer to the Hebrew text, is not without original interpretations, which can be attributed

---

[36] R. Le Déaut, "Le Targum de *Gen.* 22.8 et 1 Pt. 1.20", *RSR* 49 (1961) pp. 103-106. On the theology of the *Aqedah* (sacrifice of Isaac) and the New Testament, see G. Vermes, *Scripture and Tradition*, pp. 193-257.

[37] *Fragmentary Targum*, and *Neofiti* margin. See M. L. Klein, *The Fragment-Targums of the Pentateuch* (Analecta Biblica 76), Rome, 1980, vol. I, p. 170; vol. II, p. 129. Concerning the text, one could consult the studies of P. Winter, "Lc 2,49 and Targum Yerushalmi", *ZNW* 45 (1954) pp. 145-179; P. Grelot, "Sagesse 10,21 et le Targum de l'Exode", in *Biblica* 42 (1961) pp. 49-60.

to the theological ideas of the translator and his historical milieu. Examples of this are found in the identifications which actualize the Greek text (e.g., the "Greeks" in *Isaiah* 9.11 replace the earlier "Philistines"), and in the borrowings from an oral tradition which enriches the Scripture. We know that there are long sections which have no counterpart in the Hebrew text (as in *Esther* and *Daniel*).[38]

Every translation presupposes an interpretation. Minute alterations of the text contribute to determining the sense and the use of such and such a passage, thus orienting its exegesis for generations. From the Christian perspective, we may note the importance of the term παρθένος (meaning "virgin" instead of the ambiguous Hebrew word 'almah) in *Isaiah* 7.14. A cursory reading (or is it rather studied and deliberate?) of the Hebrew text of *Jeremiah* 31.8 ("Among them are the blind and the lame") resulted in situating the great return of the exiles and the restoration of Israel "in the feast of the Passover" (LXX 38.8). This adds a new dimension to the already rich significance of this feast.[39]

The ancient versions should not therefore be considered solely as privileged witnesses to the history and critical establishment of the sacred text (besides, witnesses not fully trustworthy, as we have seen). But rather, they must also be understood as revealing the various stages in the evolution of religious ideas. For example, by replacing "As the duration time of the trees shall be the duration time of my people" of *Isaiah* 65.22 with "*as the days of the tree of life* shall be the days of my people", the Greek and Aramaic translations witness to a doctrinal progression which is realized during the second century before our era. There is a substitution of the promise of immortality for extraordinary longevity of life. In this context, it is necessary to mention the theological evolution which

---

[38] A. Díez Macho shows the interest of studying the recension of *Tobit* in the *Codex Sinaiticus* which is much more paraphrastic than the *Vaticanus* and the *Alexandrinus*. If this is a translation from the Aramaic, then this would surely be a pre-Christian Palestinian Aramaic targum (*Mélanges E. Tisserant* vol. I, p. 185). The manuscripts of *Tobit* recovered at Qumran (three in Aramaic and one in Hebrew) follow the longer recension of the *Sinaiticus* and the *Vetus Latina*. The original language seems to have been Aramaic: J. T. Milik, *Ten Years of Discovery in the Wilderness of Judaea*, London, 1959, p. 31.

[39] Instead of *bm 'wr wpsh* the translator read *bmw'd psh* (with the "d" and "r" being easily confused). Tertullian (*De baptismo* 19.2) understood this as referring to the fifty days of the Easter season.

the translations manifest — in relation to the Hebrew text — in areas as important as the concept of God, Messianism, the role of Torah, eschatology. But this would take us beyond our subject matter.[40]

Use of the comparative method establishes that these translations often reflect very ancient exegesis, and one could wager that the authors of the New Testament interpreted the sacred texts in a way similar to them. Examples which deserve comment are far from being rare. Thus, G. Vermes has established the antiquity of the exegesis of *Exodus* 4.24-26 where the LXX and the targums all agree concerning the expiatory, sacrificial and redemptive aspects of the circumcision of Moses' child by his wife Zipporah.[41] In order to assess the possible connections between the theology of Christian baptism and Jewish circumcision it will not be sufficient simply to recover the primitive, original meaning of such an institution nor even the literal meaning for all the Old Testament texts which mention it. The expiatory meaning (which is also given to the sacrifice of the passover lamb) can be considered as an enrichment which made this "redemptive" sacrifice (since it saved Moses from death) an anticipation of the sacrifice of Christ. In this context, we can also point out the targumic presentation of the sacrifice of the covenant at *Exodus* 24.8 (cf. *Matthew* 26.28; *Mark* 14.24), where the expiatory significance of the blood poured out on the altar is made explicit (even in *Onkelos*). Thus we read:

> Moses took the blood and sprinkled (it) upon the altar (cf. *Hebrews* 12.24; *1 Peter* 1.2) *to make atonement for* (*lekappara' 'al*) the people.[42]

Nevertheless it cannot be said that in every case the translation marks a progression. Thus, in the case of the translation of the

---

[40] See the numerous examples in L. Prijs, *Jüdische Tradition in der Septuaginta*, Leiden, 1948 and read the stimulating article of D. Barthélemy, "L'Ancien Testament a mûri à Alexandrie", *TZ* 21 (1965) pp. 358-370.

[41] G. Vermes, *Scripture and Tradition in Judaism*, pp. 178-192. Again, compare the Massoretic text (MT) and the Septuagint (LXX) for *Isaiah* 8.14; *Job* 14.6; *Habakkuk* 3.2; *Deuteronomy* 26.5; *Genesis* 4.13; *Numbers* 24.7; *1 Samuel* 1.14 (cf. Philo's *De ebrietate* §146). In the very account of the miraculous origins of the LXX, the Jewish tradition listed 15 significant variants (*Meg.* 9a; cf. *Mekhilta on Exodus* 12.40).

[42] On the other hand note that this sacrifice is accomplished by the first-born of Israel (*Exodus* 24.5).

word *torah* as νόμος, the meaning of biblical revelation runs the risk of being obliterated in favor of a code of religious observances.[43] On the other hand the equivalence of *berîth-διαϑήκη* established by the LXX adds the nuance of a testament which the author of *Hebrews* (esp. in 9.15-17) will use to some advantage.[44]

The essential problem of the origin of the Greek Bible (a single text that later became diversified or originally multiple recensions which were finally unified) will not be resolved until the nature of this text has been clearly defined with regard to its function as a translation; that is, until it is clearly understood whether its ultimate purpose is a simple translation or an explanatory interpretation.[45] With regard to the difference between the Septuagint and Massoretic Psalters, "there is all the difference of a *relecture* (re-reading)... which immediately prepared the prayer of the Christian Church."[46] H. Cazelles assures us[47] that A. Gelin (with whom the term "*relecture*" is associated in France) would have preferred *reinterpretation*. In effect this is exactly what has taken place:

> the rewriting of the Bible, i.e., the introduction of a contemporary interpretation into the translation of the text.[48]

The Septuagint more often than not represents more than a translation *ad sensum*[49] ("according to the meaning"), it is actually an exegesis of the text. In fact, it seems that the translators conceived of their task as including that of commentator. Although the targums found at Qumran faithfully follow the Hebrew text (yet with some traces of "targumisms"), studies of the Aramaic versions

---

[43] However, L. Mosengwo Pasinya has demonstrated that the Greek translators did not give the equivalence *Torah-νόμος* a legalistic sense. See *La notion de Nomos dans le Pentateuque grec* (Analecta Biblica 52), Rome, 1973.

[44] A. Jaubert, *La notion d'Alliance dans le Judaïsme*, Paris, 1963, pp. 311-315.

[45] See the important review of P. Kahle's *The Cairo Geniza* by G. Vermes in *NTS* 6 (1959-1960) pp. 323-325.

[46] G. Jouassard, in *A la rencontre de Dieu*, pp. 358-359.

[47] *Ibid.*, p. 118.

[48] G. Vermes, *Scripture and Tradition in Judaism*, p. 179.

[49] Jerome writes concerning the Septuagint translation of *Isaiah* 65.22, which we cited above: "Qui magis sensum ex Hebraeo vertere quam verba" ("who translated from Hebrew the meaning rather than the words", PL 24, 649).

confirm A. Geiger's opinion that the most ancient ones are more paraphrastic in nature, and he characterized them by the following words, *Erklärung* ("explication"), *Erweiterung* ("development"), and *Ermahnung* ("exhortation"). The targums of *Deuteronomy* 1.1 offer us a good illustration of this. Only at a second stage were they revised and their texts brought into greater conformity with the Hebrew text. A. T. Olmstead formulated the principle, "...more midrashic character is surely a sign of earlier date."[50] These texts are therefore very close to midrash and possess their own "theology" (as distinct from that of the biblical text) as the few examples to be examined later will demonstrate.

The Importance of Targums

One question immediately comes to mind: haven't we already exhausted those sources which we claim are so important? The answer is no, because on the one hand Jewish scholars tended to study especially the legal or juridical texts of their tradition and were not inclined to initiate comparative studies between their haggadic inheritance and the New Testament; on the other hand, the Christians, considering that the targums which have come down to us today originated after the first century of our era, did not think that these could shed any light for interpreting the Christian sources. It seems that today this way of perceiving things is untenable. Let it suffice to recall that the research of G. Vermes, P. Grelot, A. Díez Macho, J. Heinemann and others has come to the conclusion that the recensions of the Palestinian targums have preserved many exegetical traditions which would have circulated in the Jewish community of the first century.[51]

---

[50] A. Geiger, *Urschrift und Übersetzungen der Bibel*, Berlin, 1857, p. 452; A. T. Olmstead, "Could an Aramaic Gospel be Written?" *Journal of Near Eastern Studies* 1 (1942) p. 60. The problem is far from being solved; it is the content, not the length of a paraphrase, which is to be considered in order to determine the antiquity of an exegesis. Cf. G. Vermes, in *Post-Biblical Jewish Studies*, p. 121 (= *Annual of Leeds University Oriental Society*, vol. III [1961-1962] Leiden, 1963, p. 107).

[51] Cf. P. Kahle, *ZNW* 49 (1958) p. 115. For the present state of targumic studies see M. McNamara, "Targums", *Interpreter's Dictionary of the Bible*, Supp. Vol., Nashville, 1976, pp. 856-861; R. Le Déaut, "The Current State of

The manuscript of the Aramaic Pentateuch (*Codex Neofiti 1*), discovered by Díez Macho in the Vatican Library in 1956, contains material which is probably very old. But the language (more ancient than that of the Palestinian *Talmud*, it seems) presupposes a first redaction from about the third century of our era. The manuscript itself was copied at Rome in 1504. Rabbi Menaḥem Kasher, an Israeli scholar and eminent specialist in rabbinic literature, declared that the *Neofiti* is older than all the halakic midrashim, older than the Mishnah, even several centuries older than Christianity! Moreover he dates the origin of the institution of targum to the time of Esdras.[52] This testimony is precious in the sense that an expert of the immense rabbinic literature does not find there any data that would lead one to attribute the whole content of the targum to a more recent age.

Thus we can, with some confidence, consider that the targumic sources *on the whole* represent an exegetical tradition which is at least contemporaneous to Christ. But since there are traits of a more recent date within this literature, before using a particular targumic tradition it is necessary to test its antiquity. This is a difficult task: not all the texts have critical editions,[53] concordances are lacking, and dictionaries are incomplete (and practically non-existent for the Samaritan sources). Often we can only end with a series of probabilities and solid application of the targumic riches remains a generation or two away. Contemporary critical research in this area is still in the beginning stages. Today it can be said of

---

Targumic Studies", *Biblical Theology Bulletin* 4 (1974) pp. 3-32. Among the Aramaic translations one should also mention the Samaritan targum (see J. Mac-Donald, *Memar Marqah*, Berlin, 1963, and my review in *Biblica* 46 [1965] pp. 84-87). One must also make mention of the critical edition prepared by A. Tal, *The Samaritan Targum of the Pentateuch: Part 1 Genesis, Exodus*, Tel-Aviv, 1980.

[52] In the illustrated weekly (in Hebrew) *Panim el Panim*, n. 291, 27th Nov. 1964 (Jerusalem), pp. 15-17. He devotes the whole of volume 24 of his *Torah Shelemah* (Talmudic-Midrashic Encyclopedia of the Pentateuch, Jerusalem, 1974) to targums under the title: *Aramaic Versions of the Bible. A comprehensive Study of Onkelos, Jonathan, Jerusalem Targums and the full Jerusalem Targum of the Vatican manuscript Neofiti 1.*

[53] Even the study of complete manuscripts is not sufficient because of their lateness and because they have been modified by additions which may have come from Midrashim and liturgy. One must constantly consult at the same time the divergent recensions, even when fragmentary.

targumic studies what F. Rosenthal once wrote concerning research
on ancient Aramaic vocabulary, "Es muss *gewogen* und nicht gezählt
werden" ("Now is a time of general evaluation, not detailed conclusions").[54]   However, for the study of targumic traditions Renée
Bloch has suggested a comparative method which has already proven
to be fruitful.[55]   The method consists of tracing the formation and
the paths of a given tradition in the different Jewish writings where
it is found by means of literary criticism so as to determine its oldest
form. One can also determine a *terminus ad quem* ("the latest
possible dating") by comparing these data with the ancient writings
that can be dated with certainty, such as those of Flavius Josephus,
Philo of Alexandria, Pseudo-Philo, Qumran, etc., and any other
external data. Moreover, the study of the principal traditions of a
given document makes possible the dating of the whole with some
precision. It also allows the researcher to identify the diverse layers,
and to verify their homogeneity or their complexity. Using
targumic sources is therefore entirely possible. One must hold to
the middle channel between two perils: an over-confidence which
lacks a critical sense, and an excessive distrust analogous to the
attitude which previously considered that these documents had
practically no relevance for the exegesis of the New Testament.[56]

The importance of the Aramaic versions is now generally
admitted, and studies have multiplied.[57]   A number of passages in
the New Testament have been compared with the ancient traditions
which the Targums have preserved, and it is rare that exegetes do not
at least glance at the targumic interpretations of the Old Testament
passages which they study. Thus it is generally recognized that the
targums represent an important contribution for a better understanding of Christian origins, for here are found the essential results of

_____

[54] F. Rosenthal, *Die aramaistische Forschung*, Leiden, 1964, p. 63 (reprinted from the 1939 edition).

[55] "Note méthodologique pour l'étude de la littérature rabbinique", *RSR*
(1955) pp. 194-227. See also G. Vermes, *Scripture and Tradition in Judaism*
and J. Heinemann, *Aggadah and its Development*, Jerusalem, 1974.

[56] See my "Avant-Propos" in *Targum du Pentateuque*, vol. V, Index ana-
lytique (SC 282), Paris, 1981.

[57] See the bibliography. Among those who have recognized since long ago
the value of targums for New Testament exegesis we should cite Brian Walton,
the editor of the *London Polyglot*, (1654-1657), in ch. 12 of his "Introduction", p. 85.

ancient Jewish hermeneutics, which inspired the formulation if not the very content of the Christian message. In fact:

> ...as transformative as the Christian revelation is, it none-theless draws from the Jewish tradition not only its formulas, images, its framework, but even the very substance of its concepts. On the other hand, Christianity is not linked directly with the Old Testament, as the exegesis of a St. Paul or a St. Matthew makes sufficiently clear. Rather, it is con-nected with it through the intermediary of rabbinic exegesis. To discredit this intermediate link is to bring into question the solidity of the whole chain.[58]

It has therefore been noted that the New Testament authors understood the Bible only through an interpretation that was perhaps centuries old, and an amorphous mass of Jewish traditions, from which, because of the hardships of history, only a small part has survived to our day in comparison to what must have existed. The writings of the New Testament are immersed in the Tradition of Israel and they take root therein, just as Christ is born "of their race, according to the flesh" (*Romans* 9.5). This fertile soil of Jewish tradition born from Scripture could be compared to the *materia prima* ("prime matter") of the Scholastics. It is unchangeable in its substantial mutations, unique in the multiplicity of new forms, but absolutely indispensable for explaining any change. Does not this common basis also help to explain (on a psychological level), at least partially, the possibility of the transition from the Old Law to the New as well as the true nature of their relationship?

It is therefore extremely important to take into account the intermediary function of Jewish exegesis,[59] and the intermediary step that it represents between the biblical text and the New Testa-ment. It is fairly certain that the targums represent a link between Torah and Gospel. It is within these liturgical texts that one finds

---

[58] L. Bouyer, *La Bible et L'Evangile*, p. 250. Apropos *2 Corinthians* 3.4, B. Gerhardsson (*Memory and Manuscript*, Uppsala, 1961, p. 285) underlines the importance of these links.

[59] See the methodological critique of an article by A. Feuillet by P. Grelot in *RB* (1963) p. 44 note 8, "It always seems to me necessary not to omit the intermediary function of Jewish exegesis before which the authors of the apos-tolic age had to take a stand when giving a Christian exegesis of the sacred texts". For an example of rereading the text from the background of Jewish tradition see J. Schlosser, "Les jours de Noé et de Lot. A propos de Luc XVIII, 26-30", *RB* 80 (1973) pp. 13-36.

an ancient element common to the Synagogue and the nascent Church, a solid connection between Judaism and Christianity. Both Christians and Jews of the first century of our era viewed the Bible only through such interpretations.

The works of Josephus are significant in this regard and reveal what could be the spontaneous attitude of the first Christians when faced with the sacred texts. He views the Old Testament only through the traditional haggadah. Thus, S. Rappaport was able to write a whole study entitled *Agada und Exegese bei Flavius Josephus* (Vienna, 1930). He even held that Josephus could have used Aramaic targums for the redaction of his *Jewish Antiquities*.[60] The account of the admirable conversion of Manasseh (*Jewish Antiquities* X, §§ 40-46), the typical example of the impious that the Rabbis will later quote as one of those sinners who will not be pardoned in the other world, is undoubtedly not a personal invention of the historian. Besides the allusion to the conversion of Manasseh in *2 Chronicles* 33.12-13, he must have used traditions such as those summarized in the *Prayer of Manasseh* (which is still printed in the Vulgate). Even Philo himself, despite all his originality and genius, still reveals some affinities with the popular Palestinian tradition.[61]

Targums and the New Testament

At this point a few examples will illustrate the importance of the targumic traditions for New Testament exegesis. The examples will also illustrate how recourse to only the biblical text can irremediably prevent us from grasping the full meaning of some New Testament texts when they are referring to traditional developments. A number of examples have already been suggested by various authors, but I would like to give some samples of the different

---

[60] *Op. cit.*, pp. XX-XXIII. See P. Winter, *ZNW* 45 (1954) pp. 148-154. Winter cites (p. 152) the testimony of H. St. J. Thackeray, the specialist on Josephus, who himself made such a pertinent use of the targums in his *The Relation of St. Paul to Contemporary Jewish Thought*, London, 1900.

[61] R. Bloch, *art. cit.*, p. 204; E. Stein, *Philo und der Midrasch*, Giessen, 1931; H. A. Wolfson, *Philo*, Cambridge, Mass., 1962, vol. I, p. 91. The targum mentions the four judgements of Moses several times (*Leviticus* 24.12; *Numbers* 9.8; 15.34; 27.5). It is also striking that Philo groups those four special texts to study them together (*De vita Mosis* II, §§ 192-245).

aspects of the utilization of targums. We shall start with a few obscure passages from the Pauline writings.

In *Romans* 10.6-8 Paul makes a disconcerting use of *Deuteronomy* 30.11-14:

> But righteousness based on faith says: Do not say in your heart, "Who will ascend into heaven?" (that is, to bring Christ down) or "Who will descend into the *abyss* (ἄβυσσος)?", (that is, to bring Christ up from the dead).

S. Lyonnet[62] correctly surmised that this strange exegesis is based on a targumic interpretation of which the *Codex Neofiti* is closest to the Pauline commentary:

> The Law is not in heaven, that one should say: Would that we had one like *Moses* the prophet who would ascend to heaven and fetch it for us... Nor is the Law beyond the Great Sea that one should say: Would that we had one like *Jonah* the prophet who would descend into the depths of the Great Sea and bring it up for us.[63]

The apostle, desiring to convey to the Romans that justification by faith is not difficult to attain but is close at hand, cited the

---

[62] "Saint Paul et l'exégèse juive de son temps", *Mélanges bibliques rédigés en l'honneur de André Robert*, pp. 494-506. The marginal gloss is closer to the biblical text and St. Paul: "*Who shall ascend* for us to heaven like Moses the prophet...". But the gloss concerning Jonah, with the Hebrew, only speaks of passing over beyond the Great Sea. Billerbeck lists the passage apropos *John* 3.13 (II, p. 425), but he only includes the first part of the text, the part which refers to the notion of *ascending*. This prevented him from seeing how he could have used this for *Romans* 10. On the other hand, Thackeray (*op. cit.*, pp. 187-188) kept only the notion of *descending* into the abyss and neglected the allusion to Moses. Thus we see the importance of taking into account the whole targumic context from which any element can suddenly appear in the author's exposition.

[63] See M. McNamara, *The New Testament and the Palestinian Targum to the Pentateuch* (Analecta biblica 27), Rome, 1966 (second printing, 1978), pp. 70-78 and J. A. Fitzmyer's review in *TS* 29 (1968) p. 325. A. M. Goldberg thinks that Paul did not use a targumic *text* but was familiar with the *tradition* which forms the basis for the targum (see "Torah aus der Unterwelt?" *BZ* 14 [1970] pp. 127-131). The targum of *Jonah* 2.3 speaks about "the bottom of the abyss ('r't thwm')". At verse 6 the Hebrew and the targum read *tehom/tehoma'*; *tehom* is practically always translated by ἄβυσσος in the LXX. The "Great Sea" is the Mediterranean where Jonah was thrown overboard.

passage in *Deuteronomy* which says the same thing about the Law. But he remembered the targumic exegesis and applied to Jesus what had been said of Moses and Jonah. This was easily done since from the Christian perspective both Moses and Jonah were considered as figures of Christ (*Matthew* 12.40; *Acts* 7.20-41).

Scholars have recognized in *Jannes* and *Jambres* "who opposed Moses" (*2 Tim.* 3.8) the names which the legend attributed to the Egyptian magicians mentioned in *Exodus* 7.11; 13.22, etc. According to the targum to *Exodus* 1.15; 7.11, these were even the leaders of the magicians. M. McNamara[64] has noted that the above forms of their names are to be found only in the Palestinian version, which leads one to suppose that Paul knew one or the other form of this recension. The antiquity of this tradition is sufficiently confirmed by the *Damascus Document* (V, 18-19), which provides the earliest mention of their names:

> For in the past, Moses and Aaron arose by the hand of the Prince of Lights and Belial in his cunning raised Jannes (*yḥnh*) and his brother when Israel was delivered for the first time.[65]

Certain citations which do not agree with the biblical text can be explained by recourse to the Aramaic translations, at least at the stage of the oral tradition. Thus *Ephesians* 4.8 cites *Psalm* 68.18, "Ascending on high... *he gave gifts* to men" (evidently an allusion to the sending of the Spirit by Christ), while the Hebrew is to be translated as "*you have received* men in tribute...". The Aramaic paraphrase of this Psalm (which probably formed part of the Jewish Pentecost liturgy from early on) reads as follows:

> You ascended the firmament, O Moses the prophet, you took captivity captive, you taught the words of the Law, you gave them gifts, to the children of man.[66]

---

[64] *The New Testament*, pp. 82-96; cf. Thackeray, *The Relation*, pp. 215-222 (the chapter entitled "St. Paul the Haggadist"). L. L. Grabbe challenges McNamara's conclusions in "The Jannes/Jambres Tradition in Targum Pseudo-Jonathan and its Date", *JBL* 98 (1979) pp. 393-401.

[65] Since the time of second Isaiah, the Exodus is understood as a symbol of eschatological liberation. Jannes and his brother become the servants of Balaam in the targum of *Numbers* 22.22 and the tradition seems sometimes to lose itself within these successive avatars.

[66] On this text see M. McNamara, *The New Testament*, pp. 78-81; R. Ru-

Mark 13.22, "False Christs and false prophets will arise and show signs and wonders..." is a rather free quotation of *Deuteronomy* 13.1: "If a prophet arises among you, or a dreamer of dreams, and gives you a sign or a wonder...". However the verb in the plural (δώσουσιν) and the plural forms σημεῖα καὶ τέρατα, as well as the precision, *false* prophet, are found only in the targums. The *Codex Neofiti* is here again closer to the text of the New Testament.[67] As a consequence, there is no need to refer to the later vocabulary of the primitive Church (as V. Taylor proposes)[68], and the form of the quotation may illustrate the early character of *Mark*.

Some *formulas* of the New Testament are clarified by parallels in targums. The expression "to taste the cup of death" is found nowhere else in ancient Jewish sources except in the Palestinian targum,[69] and can enrich our understanding of the background behind the use of the word *cup* in relation to the passion and the death of Jesus (*Matthew* 20.22-23; *John* 18.11; *Luke* 22.20). It is here (i.e., in the targum) that one finds the following famous sayings:

> Blessed are the breasts from which you sucked and the womb within which you lay. (*Neofiti*)[70]

> As I am merciful in heaven, so shall you be merciful on earth. (*Ps-Jonathan*)[71]

---

binkiewicz, "Ps LXVIII 19 (≒ Eph. IV.8) Another Textual Tradition or Targum?" *Novum Testamentum* 17 (1975) pp. 219-224; A. T. Hanson, *The New Testament Interpretation of Scripture*, London, 1980, p. 136.

[67] The plural of the verb in the text, *signs and wonders* (*symnyn*, from the Greek σημεῖον!) in the gloss.

[68] In his *The Gospel according to St. Mark*, London, 1955, p. 516 he writes, "The vocabulary has a later ring."

[69] Not only in the *Neofiti*, as I first wrote elsewhere (*Biblica* 43 [1962] pp. 82-86), but also in other recensions of the Targum (as is pointed out by S. Speier in *Vetus Testamentum* 13 [1963] pp. 344-345). M. Black has shown the interest of this expression in *Expository Times* 59 (1947-1948) p. 195 and his *An Aramaic Approach to the Gospels and Acts*[3], p. 298. The expression "cup of death" is also found in the *Testament of Abraham* XVI; cf. S. Légasse, *NTS* 20 (1974) p. 164.

[70] *Luke* 11.2/*Genesis* 49.25. On this text and the following see McNamara, *The New Testament*, pp. 131-138.

[71] *Luke* 6.36/*Leviticus* 22.28 (*rḥmn*/οἰκτίρμων). Compare *Jer. Talmud Meg.* IV,9,75c; *Ber.* V,3,9c.

The rare Palestinian targumic fragments furnished with ancient vocalization contain the word *Rabbuni* ("Teacher!"). This pronunciation is in full agreement with the gospel texts of *Mark* 10.51 and *John* 20.16, while the later current vocalization is *ribbôni*.[72]

In the targum passage for *Numbers* 20.29 Aaron is called the "pillar of the prayer of the children of Israel". This passage should be added to the rabbinic texts which Billerbeck cites to illustrate *Galatians* 2.9; *Revelation* 3.12 and *1 Timothy* 3.15. In the latter text the formula "pillar and support of the truth" occurs, and it was noted that this formula is better applied to Timothy than to "the Church of the living. God" (mentioned in the context).[73] One should note that in this passage Aaron is called a pillar because as High Priest "he made expiation for them once a year" and, according to 21.1, the pillar of luminous cloud had been given to Israel because of him. It is difficult to believe that such interpretations, often recalled in the liturgy, would not have surfaced in the consciousness of the New Testament authors. Let us point out one more gloss from the *Neofiti* (as a parallel, without any claim of dependence). Just as Jesus chooses witnesses to his miracles and especially to his Resurrection (cf. *Acts* 1.21-22), similarly Moses is said to take great care to ensure that there will be a witness to all the wonders which God had accomplished in favor of Israel during the exodus. The Hebrew text of *Numbers* 10.31 has Moses addressing Hobab, the guide for the Israelite caravan: "Do not leave us. For

---

[72] On this problem see S. Schulz, "Die Bedeutung der neuen Targumforschung für die synoptische Tradition", in *Abraham unser Vater*, p. 432. There are several examples of *rabbun* in manuscript A (the most ancient) from Cairo, cf. P. Kahle, *Masoreten des Westens*, vol. II, Stuttgart, 1930, p. 1. On this problem see also P. Kahle, *The Cairo Geniza*[2], Oxford, 1959, p. 204; M. Black, *An Aramaic Approach*[3], pp. 23, 44-46. It can be objected that this vocalization is also found in Hebrew liturgical texts, cf. E. Y. Kutscher in *ZNW* 51 (1960) pp. 52-53; N. Wieder in *Leshonenu* 27-28 (1963-1964) pp. 214-217. The constant fluctuation in the vocalization (and pronunciation?) between *a/i* and *o/u* in the targumic manuscripts encourages us to be reserved in our judgment.

[73] This interpretation is defended by A. Jaubert, "L'image de la colonne (1 Timothée 3.15)", in *Studiorum paulinorum congressus...*, vol. II (Analecta biblica 18), Rome, 1963, pp. 101-108. Cf. R. D. Aus, "Three Pillars and Three Patriarchs: A Proposal concerning Gal. 2.9", *ZNW* 70 (1979) pp. 252-261; R. Le Déaut, "Aspects de l'intercession dans le Judaïsme ancien", *JSJ* 1 (1970) pp. 35-37. For the meaning of "column" in the sense of "potentate" see *Targum Genesis* 46.28; 49.19; *Exodus* 15.14,15.

you know the regions where we must camp in the desert and you therefore will be our eyes." The targum (*Neofiti*) explains:

> Please do not leave us. Because you know the marvels that the Lord has worked with us... in the wilderness; you shall be a testimony for us.[74]

In his commentary on the Beatitude of the pure in heart (*Matthew* 5.8), Billerbeck (I, p. 214) affirms that there is not a single passage within rabbinic literature which makes the vision of God depend on purity of heart. Whatever the precise meaning of the Beatitude of the gospel, one could add to the debate this targumic commentary concerning *Leviticus* 9.6 ("This is what YHWH has commanded of you to do so that his glory will appear to you"):[75] "Put away the evil inclination from your hearts (= *Sifra*) and at once will be revealed to you the Glory of the Shekinah of the Lord" (i.e., you will see the Lord).

Without wanting to establish a literary dependence between the two texts, we nevertheless think it interesting to compare the last of the Matthean beatitudes (*Matthew* 5.11-12) with the oracle of Balaam (who was bribed to curse Israel).[76] The Matthean text reads:

> Blessed are you when men revile you <Vulgate: *curse you*>... Rejoice and be glad for your reward is great *in heaven*.

The oracle of Balaam reads:

> Happy are you O righteous ones! What a good reward is prepared for you before the Lord for the world to come!

---

[74] The midrash *Sifre on Numbers* emphasizes that Hobab could not abandon Israel because *he saw with his own eyes* the wonders (=Onkelos!) in the desert. K. G. Kuhn's *Sifre zu Numeri*, Stuttgart, 1959, p. 211 refers to *John* 2.23 and *Matthew* 11.20-24.

[75] In 9.5 it is said that the people "stood with perfect heart (*blb šlym*) before the Lord". Before revealing to them the mysteries of the future Jacob demanded of his sons that they purify themselves of all impurities (in the ritual sense) in *Genesis* 49.1 (*Ps-Jonathan*). Moreover, by abstaining from conjugal activity, Moses ensured his intimacy with God (*Ps-Jonathan* targum for *Numbers* 12. 2, 8; *Deuteronomy* 5.31).

[76] Notice that the verb being used by Matthew ὀνειδίζω means "to insult, to reproach someone". Yet the Greek text in the Balaam episode only uses ἀρᾶσθαι/καταρᾶσθαι, verbs which in the *Septuagint* never render the same Hebrew verbs as ὀνειδίζω.

The above is the *Neofiti* text (for *Numbers* 23.23), but other recensions are more precise: "...<the reward> is prepared for you with your Father *in heaven*, for the world to come".[77] The notion of "the least in the kingdom of Heaven" (*Matthew* 11.11) is expressed equivalently by the same Balaam in all the Palestinian recensions of *Numbers* 23.10:

> Were Israel to kill him by the sword, Balaam proclaims that he does not have a portion in the world to come. However, were Balaam to die the death of the upright, would that his end were like that of *the smallest among them.*

*
*   *

Often enough it is not only on the level of some typical formula but on a much larger scale that there is a correspondence between the New Testament and Jewish Tradition. Thus when the evangelists or St. Paul tell us about Adam, Abraham, Moses, Elijah, etc. (that is, of personalities from the history of Israel), should we think that they imagined them as we do, according to the often succinct data of the Old Testament? Evidently not. All historical personalities have their legends (especially in the sphere of religion), and in forming this image that we all have of great people of the past, a novel or a fine film is often more important than the learned work of an historian. When the heroes from the history of Israel appear in the New Testament, we should therefore imagine them according to these sketches derived from popular tradition. When Matthew names Tamar within his genealogy as one of Christ's ancestors, this is probably not to insinuate because of the questionable past of this person, that Christ had come to save sinners (which was the common opinion since Jerome). It was rather because, in conformity to the Jewish tradition, for which the targum is the most authoritative witness: "He saw in Tamar not only an ancestor of Christ, but a woman who had ardently desired this favor and wanted to participate in the

---

[77] See M. L. Klein, *The Fragment-Targums*, vol. I, pp. 104 and 202. Biller-beck (vol. I, pp. 231-232) does not mention this targumic text. None of his references actually speak of a reward "in heaven", but only in the other world. It must however be noted that "Father who (is) in heaven" is a usual formula.

messianic blessings."[78]   And because of this, under heavenly inspiration, she had seduced her father-in-law, as is well known (*Genesis* 38): "A voice came forth from heaven and said: Both are righteous. From before YHWH the thing has come about". In this way the *Neofiti* text (38.25) summarizes the profound meaning of the whole event. For Philo, Tamar becomes the model for all proselytes (*De Virtutibus* §§221-222), and he gives the following greatly idealized eulogy:

> She kept her own life stainless and was able to win the good report (εὐφημία) which belongs to the good.[79]

The biblical text itself attests to analogous phenomena of transfiguration, and A. Jaubert makes the following remark concerning the eulogy of Levi in *Malachi* 2.4-8:

> This panegyric of Levi is unique in the Hebrew Bible, ... truth, righteousness and peace..., it would be hard to contradict more the account of *Genesis* (34; cf. 49.5-7). We must believe that there were common midrashic accounts on Levi that portrayed him in completely different colors![80]

---

[78] R. Bloch, "Judah engendra Pharès et Zara de Thamar", (*Matthew* 1.3) in *Mélanges A. Robert*, pp. 381-389. In contrast to Reuben's story, the Mishnah (*Megillah* IV,10) gives permission to read and comment on the history of Tamar. According to H. Stegemann, the common denominator between the women in the Matthean genealogy is that they are "pagan": "'Die des Uria' — Zur Bedeutung der Frauennamen in der Genealogie von Matthäus 1,1-17", in *Tradition und Glaube* (Festschrift K. G. Kuhn), Göttingen, 1971, pp. 246-276. M. Smith suggests an apologetic intention in *Palestinian Parties and Politics that Shaped the Old Testament*, New York/London, 1971, pp. 162 and 266. Cf. also W. D. Davies, *The Setting of the Sermon on the Mount*, Cambridge, 1964, p. 288. One can find much useful information in the article entitled "RAHAB" in the *DBS*, vol. IX, 1086-1092 (F. Langlamet).

[79] Scandalized, F. L. Colson comments, "This beatification of the actress in what to our minds is a peculiarly shocking story outdoes the other extravagances of the *De Nobilitate*" (Philo, vol. VIII, 1954, p. 450). In the *Biblical Antiquities* of Ps-Philo (IX,5) one reads from the mouth of Moses' father, Amram, a moving eulogy of "our mother Thamar — mater nostra Thamar". It is clear that the ancients would also be shocked by our myopic interpretation of the Scriptures.

[80] *La notion d'Alliance dans le Judaïsme*, p. 38.

As with Tamar, the other women in the genealogy of Matthew were also "canonized" by the tradition. Rahab, the prostitute of Jericho (*Joshua* 2.1), was depicted as a model of faith (cf. *Hebrews* 11.31; *James* 2.25), as gifted with the spirit of prophecy (Josephus, *Jewish Antiquities* V, §12), as mother of kings and of prophets, among whom were Jeremiah and Ezekiel! A critical sorting would have to be made among all the Jewish texts concerning her (Billerbeck, I, pp. 20-23), but the witness of the New Testament is sufficient to suggest an ancient date for the process of "rehabilitation". And this is perhaps also to be seen in the fact that the targum, as well as Josephus, substitutes "innkeeper" for the term "harlot" which is found in the Hebrew and Greek texts.[81] Within the Christian tradition Rahab becomes a figure of the Church.[82] As for Ruth, we know that she enjoyed great renown as the ancestor of king David and therefore of the Messiah.[83]

Among the ancestors of the Messiah, a special place should be made for Miriam, the sister of Moses and Aaron. In fact, it seems that first century Jews had a conception of her that exceeded by far the very limited data on her in the biblical accounts. We know of her role in saving Moses (*Exodus* 2.4-10) and the embarrassing episode of *Numbers* 12 which *Deuteronomy* 24.9 recalls without commenting. But it is surprising to see her mentioned among the guides of the people of God in *Micah* 6.4:

> For I brought you up from the land of Egypt, and redeemed you from the house of bondage; and I sent before you Moses, Aaron and Miriam.

The targumic commentaries rival each other in presenting her as the one who announces the birth of Moses, in insisting on her role in Egypt, and even in counting her among the midwives who receive as reward membership in "a house of kingship and a house

---

[81] S. Rappaport, *op. cit.*, p. 40.

[82] J. Daniélou, *Sacramentum futuri*, Paris, 1950, pp. 217-232. "Typo meretrix, mysterio ecclesia" (St. Ambrose). See F. Langlamet's "RAHAB" in *DBS*, vol. IX, 1065-1092.

[83] Billerbeck, vol. I, pp. 23-27; J. B. Bauer, "Das Buch Ruth in der jüdischen und christlichen Überlieferung" in *Bibel und Kirche* 18 (1963) pp. 116-119; D. Daube, *The New Testament and Rabbinic Judaism*, pp. 27-36.

of high-priesthood". From Miriam (according to *Neofiti Exodus* 1.21) who receives the crown of royalty, king David and the future Messiah will be born. She participates in the suffering of the people in the desert, and it is because of her that YHWH gives Israel the well (or the rock) which will follow Israel in all of its wanderings (*1 Corinthians* 10.4). Alongside Moses, she holds a position of first importance and is not only "the sister of the chief" (ἀδελφὴ τοῦ στρατηγοῦ) (see Josephus, *Jewish Antiquities* III, §105), but one of the "three pastors" or "faithful chiefs" of the people of God which Joseph saw in a figurative way in the three small branches on the vine in *Genesis* 40.10.[84] Is there not, in this legend of Miriam, a starting point for the place Christian theology will assign to Mary (whose name seems intentionally chosen), at the side of Jesus, the new Moses? Research in this area should take into account the developments of the haggadah and not forget, for example, that if Miriam is called *ha-'almah* in *Exodus* 2.8 (as in the famous passage of *Isaiah* 7.14), she was then considered primarily as the ancestor of David, a more significant detail for any eventual parallel than the "virginity" which could be suggested by the text of Exodus.

*
*   *

When studying the connections between Targum and New Testament, one must go beyond the verbal ties and consider the whole of the tradition. This approach is particularly indispensable in the case of episodes from the Old Testament to which the authors of the New Testament seem to refer. A number of studies[85] have brought to light the importance of the sacrifice of Isaac in ancient Jewish thought. Tradition situates the sacrifice of Isaac on the same day as the Passover (cf. *Jubilees* 17-18) on Mt. Zion. It is recalled each year as a sacrifice which merits for Israel pardon of its sins and

---

[84] One can find ample development in "Miryam, soeur de Moïse, et Marie, mère du Messie", *Biblica* 45 (1964) pp. 198-219.

[85] G. Vermes, *Scripture and Tradition in Judaism*, pp. 193-227; R. Le Déaut, *La nuit pascale*, pp. 131-212; S. Spiegel, *The Last Trial*, New York, 1967; R. J. Daly, "The Soteriological Significance of the Sacrifice of Isaac", *CBQ* 39 (1977) pp. 45-47; J. Swetnam, *Jesus and Isaac: A Study of the Epistle to the Hebrews in the Light of the Aqedah* (Analecta Biblica 94), Rome, 1981. See the challenging positions of P. R. Davies, B. D. Chilton, "The Aqedah: A Revised Tradition History", *CBQ* 40 (1978) pp. 514-546.

salvation. It became the very type of sacrifice which pleases the Lord and which He rewards. The liturgical commentaries of this "Passover story" prepared the mind to understand the gift of the Father who also gave his only begotten (cf. *John* 3.16; *Romans* 8.32).

Recently, A. Jaubert utilized a collection of targumic legends centered around the miraculous well of Harran (*Genesis* 29), an overflowing well which Jacob presents the shepherds of Laban, to illustrate the meaning of *John* 4, which takes place near the "well of Jacob".[86]

When one comments on *John* 3.14, the allusion to the bronze serpent which "Moses lifted up in the desert" (*Numbers* 21.4-9), the figure of Christ lifted up and glorified on the cross, one goes at first to the midrash in the book of *Wisdom* (16.6-14).[87]   The biting of the serpents was allowed by God so as to bring the Israelites back to His Law (this is important), and they were saved not because they turned their eyes towards the suspended serpent (σύμβολον σωτη-ρίας) but towards God, the universal Savior. This interpretation is also found in the Aramaic translations and in the rabbinic writings (*Mekhilta Exodus* 17.11; *Rosh ha-Shanah* III,8). But the targums of *Numbers* 21.4 unanimously mention the presence of an important figure: the serpent which bites the Hebrews is the serpent of *Genesis* (the word for serpent is singular in *Neofiti*), the ancient serpent (see also *Revelation* 12.9; 20.2), Satan, whose place as leader of the sons of darkness in the gospel of John is well known. This is a kind of concretization of the commentary which the targum gives us of *Genesis* 3.15:[88]

---

[86] "La symbolique du puits de Jacob", in *L'homme devant Dieu* (*Mélanges offerts au Père Henri de Lubac*), vol. I, Paris, 1964, pp. 63-73. Cf. Targum *Genesis* 28.10. For the traditions on the water and the well in Jewish interpretation see G. Bienaimé, *Moïse et le don de l'eau au désert*, Diss. Biblical Institute, Rome, 1981 (to be published under the title *Moïse et le don de l'eau dans la tradition juive ancienne: targum et midrash* in the series "Analecta Biblica" by the Biblical Institute Press, Rome).

[87] On the connections between the gospel of John and *Wisdom* see G. Ziener, *Biblica* 38 (1957) pp. 396-416; 39 (1958) pp. 37-60. More recently see the exhaustive study of H. Maneschg, *Die Erzählung von der ehernen Schlange (Num. 21.4-9) in der Auslegung der frühen jüdischen Literatur*, Frankfurt A.M./ Bern, 1981.

[88] This association was facilitated by the presence of the same word *serpent* in both passages and, − in the same two contexts − *the nourishment* of the Hebrews (the manna) and that of the serpent (the earth) (see *Genesis* 3.14).

I will put enmity between you and the woman, and between your sons and her sons. And it will come to be that when her sons observe the Torah and put into practice the commandments they will aim at you and strike you on your head and kill you. But when they forsake the commandments of the Torah[89] you will take aim and bite him <them?> on his heel <their heels?> and afflict him <them?>. However, for her sons <read *bnyh*> there will be a remedy, whereas for you, O serpent, there will be no remedy, for they will make peace at the end, in the day of King Messiah.

We have translated the *Neofiti*[90] recension which presents passages which are obscure and undoubtedly corrupt.

In order not to overestimate the implications of this enigmatic text, let it suffice to say that, as in *Wisdom*, victory over the serpent is conditional to returning to the Law. It is possible that the author of *Wisdom* was connecting the scene of *Numbers* with that of *Genesis* 3, viewed through midrashic elaboration. We know that for Philo the serpent of bronze which healed is the replica of the evil serpent which tempted Eve.[91] Moreover it is interesting to note a curious literary encounter. *Wisdom* opposes the lot of the Egyptians who "were dying from being bitten ($\delta\acute{\eta}\gamma\mu\alpha\tau\alpha$, cf. *Numbers* 21.6: $\check{\epsilon}\delta\alpha\kappa\nu o\nu$) by locusts and flies(!) without ever finding a remedy to save them" to the lot of the Hebrews: "Regarding *your sons*, even the teeth of poisonous serpents would not be effective, your mercy came to their aid and saved them" (16. 9-10). We leave to the specialists of the Fourth Gospel the task of telling us to what extent the targumic exegesis of *Genesis* 3 and *Numbers* 21 has left its traces on the Johannine writings. Indeed in *John* 3 there is no literary indication that would orient us in this direction.[92] It is possible, never-

---

[89] This is a general rule often expressed in the targums: Israel will triumph when it is faithful to the Torah (*Genesis* 25.23; 27.22, 40; *Numbers* 24.14; *Deuteronomy* 33.29).

[90] One could examine the recensions of the *Fragmentary Targum* in M. L. Klein, *The Fragment-Targums*, vol. II, pp. 7 and 91. The problem of the messianic connotation cannot be dealt with here.

[91] *Leg. Alleg.* II, §81 cited by C. H. Dodd, *The Interpretation of the Fourth Gospel*, Cambridge, 1955, p. 306.

[92] Is there not an indication of use of Jewish tradition in the commentary of Aphrahat: "Nobis seipsum Jesus adfixit (cruci), ut in ipsum intuentes effugeremus plagas serpentis qui est Satanas" ("Jesus suspended himself [from the cross] for us so that in fixing our eyes upon him we would be saved from the wounds of the serpent, who is Satan", *Patrologia syriaca*, vol. I, p. 523).

theless, that John (as in *Revelation*) was thinking about the role of
Satan in the story of the first sin, especially as certain authors admit
an allusion to the woman of Genesis in the words of Jesus on the
cross: "Woman, here is your son" (19.26). The promise of the
healing "during the days of the King Messiah" is realized for the
believers: "so that whoever believes in him may have eternal life"
(*John* 3.15). What Christ brings to the world is no longer healing
from the bite of a serpent, but liberation from the curse of death
introduced into the world by "the envy of the Devil" (*Wisdom*
2.24). The evangelist of the *Logos* could not have been ignorant
of the conclusion of the midrash in *Wisdom* (16.12):

> For neither herb nor poultice cured them, but it was your
> word, O Lord, which heals all men. (δ $\sigma \delta s$, $\kappa \dot{\upsilon} \rho \iota \epsilon$, $\lambda \delta \gamma o s$ δ
> $\pi \dot{\alpha} \nu \tau \alpha s$ $\dot{\iota} \dot{\omega} \mu \epsilon \nu o s$)

Another targumic commentary of *Genesis* 5.3 was compared to
various Johannine texts by J. Ramón Díaz.[93]   The Hebrew reads:

> When Adam had lived one hundred and thirty years, he
> became the father of a son in his own likeness, after his
> image, and named him Seth.

The *Jerusalem Bible* offers the following note on this verse: "Likeness to God is therefore a quality of human nature, which the first
man passes on to his descendants."   This origin assures every person
a kind of "divine filiation", as is suggested in the genealogy of *Luke*
3.38, "...the son of Enosh, the son of Seth, the son of Adam, the
son of God".   According to *Genesis* 5.3, "Adam became the father
of a son in his own likeness, after his image, and named him Seth."
Ps-Jonathan specifies that the son was "like to his portrait"[94] and
adds:

---

[93] "Palestinian Targum and the New Testament", *Novum Testamentum* 6
(1963) 79 (which appeared in Spanish in *Estudios Bíblicos* 22 [1962] pp. 337-
342).   See also N. A. Dahl, "Der Erstgeborene Satans und der Vater des Teufels
(Polyk. 7.1 und Joh. 8.44)", in *Apophoreta* (Fest. E. Haenchen), Berlin, 1964,
pp. 70-84.

[94] The semitic word 'qwn comes from the Greek $\epsilon \dot{\iota} \kappa \dot{\omega} \nu$ = likeness, por-
trait, iconic statue (Jastrow).   On that which follows see the commentary of
J. Bowker, *The Targums*, pp. 136 and 142; A. M. Goldberg, "Kain: Sohn des
Menschen oder Sohn der Schlange?" *Judaica* 25 (1969) pp. 203-221.

For before that, Eve had borne Cain who was not from him (Adam) and was not like to him and Abel was killed at the hands of Cain. And Cain was cast out and his descendance was not enrolled in the book of the genealogy of Adam. And after that there was born one who was like him and he called his name Seth.

The text appears to suggest that the reason Cain killed his brother (and Ramón Díaz neglected this detail) is because he was not born of Adam (and therefore he was not born of God). In fact the manuscript *Add. 27031* of the *British Library* (fol. 7a) in effect reads in the following manner at *Genesis* 4.1: "Adam knew his wife *who was already pregnant (mt'br')* by Sammael, the angel of YHWH."[95] This Sammael, called the angel of death, intervened in the temptation of Eve (*Genesis* 3.6) and is explicitly identified as Satan in later Jewish tradition.[96]

In this context, listen to Jesus speak out against his adversaries (*John* 8.37-44):

> Yes I know that you are Abraham's descendants; nevertheless you want to kill me... You do the works of your father... If God were your father, you would love me... You are the children of your father, the Devil, and you want to do your father's desires. He was a murderer from the very beginning...

The first epistle of *John* (3.8-12) is still more explicit:

> He who commits sin belongs to the Devil...; no one born of God commits sin, for God's nature (σπέρμα) abides in him and he cannot sin because he is born of God. By this it may

---

[95] *Editio princeps* (Venice 1591): "And Adam knew Eve, his wife, who had desired (*ḥmd*) the angel. And she conceived and bare Cain".

[96] References are found in L. Ginzberg, *The Legends of the Jews*, vol. VI, Philadelphia, 1928, p. 159. The targum of *Job* (28.7) also mentions Sammael in relation to Eve and the tree of life. See also *4 Maccabees* 18.9; *3 Baruch* 9.7 in R. H. Charles, *Apocrypha and Pseudepigrapha*, vol. II, pp. 538 and 684; Ginzberg, *The Legends*, V, p. 133. It should be remembered how much Jewish tradition was conscious of the continuous action of Satan in the whole history of the chosen people (cf. L. Ginzberg, *The Legends*, vol. VII, pp. 414-415 and 418-419). He is also constantly present in the background of the New Testament, see S. Lyonnet, *Dictionnaire de Spiritualité*, III, pp. 142-152.

be seen who are the children of God, and, who are the
children of the Devil... We must love one another... Be not
like Cain *who was of the evil one* and murdered his brother.[97]

These examples demonstrate that the authors of the New Testament, in referring to a particular passage of the Old Testament, were
conscious of its haggadic background and not only of the Hebrew
original texts or their translations (be they Greek or Aramaic, depend-
ing on the case at hand). The various elements of this tradition
spring easily into their minds and could unexpectedly enter into the
explanation. It is, therefore, necessary to study the whole theme in
question and not just certain verbal similarities within the New Testament text. Concerning *Romans* 7, S. Lyonnet has demonstrated
how much clearer Pauline formulae become when placed in the larger
context of the Jewish conception of Adam and Moses.[98] I have also
attempted to demonstrate that a whole set of targumic data can help
understand entire sections such as *Galatians* 4.29-30 or *2 Corinthians*
3.7-18.[99] In the case of the Jesus/Moses typology, as R. Bloch has
well illustrated[100], there is a rich collection of references which one
must keep in mind to grasp the meaning of numerous allusions found
in the Gospels or the *Acts*. The Pauline reaction to "trust in works"
(*Romans* 10.3; *Philippians* 3.9) is better understood when we re-
peatedly see such a confidence expressed in the commentaries developed within the synagogue (see *Targum Exodus* 13.18; *Numbers*
31.50; *Deuteronomy* 16.16 etc.).[101] If Paul had known a Palestinian
targum analogous to the *Neofiti*, how would he have reacted to the
systematic substitutions of *"the love of the Law"* for *"the love of
God"* in all of *Deuteronomy*?[102]

---

[97] For another example concerning the use of haggadah on Cain and Abel
see *Biblica* 42 (1961) pp. 30-36 and the article by G. Vermes in *The Annual of
Leeds University* 3 (1961-1962) pp. 81-114. L. Bloy calls Cain the *"patriarche
des tueurs"* ("patriarch of the murderers") (*Le salut par les Juifs*, XXVI).

[98] *Biblica* 43 (1962) pp. 117-151.

[99] *Biblica* 42 (1961) pp. 17-47.

[100] In *Moïse, l'homme de l'Alliance*, pp. 161-166.

[101] Needless to say this has to be situated within a complex context and we
should abstain from unjustly associating Judaism with legalism. See the rectifi-
cation of E. P. Sanders, *Paul and Palestinian Judaism*, London, 1977 and B. S.
Jackson, "Legalism", *JJS* 30 (1979) pp. 1-21.

[102] So *Deuteronomy* 6.5; 10.12; 11.1, 13, 22; 13.4; 30.6, 16, 20. But
probably some of these are later rabbinic editing.

The very peculiar use of *Memra dYHWH* ("Word of YHWH") for speaking about the actions of God who constantly intervenes in the salvation history (a use which reveals more than a banal concern to avoid an anthropomorphism) is surely a more enlightening explanation for the Johannine prologue than the references to the Hellenistic *Logos*. The habit of hearing this formula time and time again in the commentaries of the synagogue provided a starting point for the preaching of the doctrine of the *Word* in circles which were rigorously monotheistic. A. Díez Macho has shown that a single verse from *John* (1.14) succeeded in grouping the three terms which were commonly used in the liturgy to present the divine actions, namely *Memra, Shekinah* (dwelling-presence) and *Iqar* (glory):

> The *Word* (Memra) was made flesh and dwelt among us (He made his Shekinah dwell among us) and we have beheld his *glory*.[103]

*

* *

A final point merits comment. Frequently the Aramaic translations represent real theological progress (especially in so far as explicitation is concerned) when compared to the Hebrew text. As such, they form one stage towards the revelation of the New Testament. But what they present is an "illustrated" theology. Take, for example, what the Bible tells us concerning God who is named "the one who forgives sins" (*Numbers* 14.18). Ever since the countless times God called it to conversion (especially by the voice of the prophets: *Ezekiel* 18.23,32; 33.11 etc...), Israel knew that YHWH is indeed a patient God, who "forgives iniquity and transgression and sin..." (*Exodus* 34.7-9; cf. *Psalm* 86.15). But

---

[103] *Mélanges E. Tisserant*, vol. I, pp. 171-172. Díez Macho translates as follows: "U-*Memra* biśra 'it'abed wĕ-'aśré Šekinteh bēnan wa-aḥminan yat-Yqreh". See M. McNamara, "*Logos* in the Fourth Gospel and *Memra* of the Palestinian Targum (*Exodus* 12.42)", *Expository Times* 79 (1968) pp. 115-117; *Targum and Testament*, pp. 101-106. On this very much debated problem see the critical point of view offered by J. A. Fitzmyer in *NTS* 20 (1974) pp. 394-396. See the Bibliography in *Targum du Pentateuque*, vol. I, Paris, 1978, p. 75.

commentators delight in showing this mercifulness at work in the
whole of history, and the texts of the New Testament do not forget
this concrete application. Here are some targumic examples which,
as we shall see, are confirmed by *Wisdom* before they are used again
by the New Testament.

God says to Cain (*Neofiti Genesis* 4.7):

> If you perform your deeds well in this world, it shall be
> *loosed and forgiven* you in the world to come. But if you
> do not perform your deeds well in this world, until the day
> of the great judgement your sin shall be retained (*ntyr*).[104]

Cain, for his part, addresses God in the following manner
(4.13):

> My sins are too great to bear; but it is possible before you to
> *loose and forgive*.[105]

The one hundred and twenty years mentioned in *Genesis* 6.3
are commented on in the following manner (at 7.4):

> Behold I have given them an extension of one hundred and
> twenty years, in case they might do repentance and they did
> not do it.[106]

Then we see the Lord once again conceding seven more days of
delay before releasing the waters of the deluge, still waiting for a
conversion *in extremis* ("at the last moment"). It is interesting to

---

[104] See the comparison with *Matthew* 16.19 and *John* 20.23 made by A.
Díez Macho, *ibid.*, p. 163, 178 and G. Vermes in *The Annual of Leeds University* 3 (1961-1962) pp. 107-111 (=*Post-Biblical Studies*, pp. 121-126). Díez-Macho also notes the use of the hendiadys *šry w šbq* (meaning forgiveness, more literally, "to untie and forgive") in the targums. The verb *šbq* also expresses forgiveness of sins in the Targum of *Job* from Qumran (11 Qtg*Job* 44,9).

[105] Some versions (Onkelos/LXX) have understood the verb *nasa'* in the sense of to forgive and not in the sense of to bear. The *Codex Neofiti* restores the original sense so as to comment on the verse as meaning God's patience and forgiveness (id. *Ps-Jonathan* which also speaks of Cain's conversion, *Genesis* 4.24).

[106] Compare *Mekhilta Exodus* 15.6 cited by J. Bowker, *The Targums*, p. 156. This interpretation is also known by Aphrahat in *Patrologia Syriaca*, vol. I, pp. 66, 323; vol. II, p. 55.

note that in his *Liber quaestionum hebraicarum in Genesim* Jerome shows a certain predilection towards this theological interpretation of the deluge, since he affirms that in *Genesis* 6.3 one must not translate *yādôn* with *permanebit* "shall not abide" (which nevertheless is the Vulgate reading), but rather with *judicabit* ("my spirit shall not judge forever"). He comments:

> So as not to appear cruel by not allowing sinners a chance to repent, (God) adds: "*His days will be one hundred and twenty years,*" that is, they will have one hundred and twenty years to repent. It is not human life which has been expanded to one hundred and twenty years, as many mistakenly think. Rather, (it means that) to this generation one hundred and twenty years have been given for the purpose of repenting.

The same patient mercy of God is exercised towards Sodom (*Neofiti Genesis* 18.21):

> If they ask to do penance and they expect their evil works may not be manifested before me, behold they are before me *as if I did not know them.*

And before raining down fire and sulphur on the town, YHWH sent (*Ps-Jonathan* 19.24) "showers of favor to the intent that they might work repentance, but they did not do so."

In the same way, basing itself on *Ezekiel* 33.11 and *Isaiah* 42. 21, the midrash[107] explains that God, whose desire is above all to justify (make just) his creatures and not to condemn them, tried to convert Adam after his disobedience, since it is written: "*And he addressed Adam*" (*Genesis* 3.9). The invitation to repent was seen in v. 19:

> From the sweat of your brow will you eat bread, until you *return* (or, "until you are *converted*", if one separates the word *shub* from what follows it). This *return* is to be understood as a reference to penance. But Adam was not converted, and God therefore expelled him from Paradise.

---

[107] According to a recension of *Leviticus Rabbah* at 13.2 cited in the *Pugio Fidei*, Paris, 1651, p. 455 (Leipzig edition, 1687, p. 568).

Let us now compare the midrash of *Wisdom* to these data, singling out those texts which treat God's action in regard to the Egyptians:

> *You shut your eyes* to the sins of men so that they may repent (11.23)... So, *little by little* you correct those who stumble: you caution them and remind them of the ways in which they sin so that they will turn away from evil (12.2)... In striking them *gradually* you allow room for repentance. Yet you did not ignore their natural perversity, their innate malice (12.10).

This last passage applies to the Egyptians what *Genesis* said about the perverse generation of the deluge (6.5, 12), by interpreting the intervals in the punishment, as did the targum, as an invitation to repentance.[108]

We must now read *Romans* 2.4-5 and compare:

> Or do you presume upon the riches of his kindness and forbearance and patience? Do you not know that God's kindness is meant to lead you to repentance? But by your hard and impenitent heart you are storing up wrath for yourself on the day of wrath when God's righteous *judgement* will be revealed.

Or *1 Peter* 3.20:

> ...those who formerly did not obey, when God's *patience waited* in the days of Noah, during the building of the ark...

And *2 Peter* 3.9:

> The Lord is not slow about his promise as some count slowness, but *is forbearing* toward you, not wishing that any should perish, but that all should reach repentance.

---

[108] The parallels between *Wisdom* and the Palestinian targum merit a detailed study, cf. *Genesis* 3.22//*Wisdom* 10.1; *Exodus* 12.42//*Wisdom* 18.6, 14, 16; *Exodus* 15.2//*Wisdom* 10.21; *Exodus* 15.19//*Wisdom* 19.7. One would find the same theological elaboration in certain Apocrypha such as the *Prayer of Manasseh*. This prayer was written in about the same period as the *Shemoné 'Esré* (see the sixth benediction). It was not written to glorify Manasseh but to exalt the mercy of God by using an extreme case (see P. Winter, *ZNW* 45 [1954] p. 149).

We see that the Jewish haggadah[109] provided ample material to answer the invitation of Clement of Rome (*1 Corinthians* 7):

> Let us go through all the generations and observe that from one generation to another the Master "has afforded an opportunity of repentance" (*Wisdom* 12.10) to those who are willing to turn to him. Noah preached repentance and those who heeded him were saved.[110]

One can easily grasp how the ancient interpretations, transmitted in the synagogues of Palestine and the diaspora, prepared the transition from the Bible to the Gospel, for example, from the saying of *Ezekiel* 18.23,32: "Have I any pleasure in the death of the wicked" to the proclamation of the joy in heaven at the return of a single sinner (*Luke* 15.7). This more profound penetration into the mystery of God, revealed by means of His Word, prepared the coming of the *Word* (*Hebrews* 1.1). It would only be fitting to find in the most ancient Jewish texts a *Praeparatio evangelica* ("preparation for the Gospel"),[111] and perhaps we would have a more accurate idea of the first century Jewish world, of these humble and "poor", whom we see at the threshhold of the Gospels awaiting the "consolation of Israel".

Although the midrashic and talmudic literature has preserved a quantity of ancient materials, it is closely associated with the scholar-

---

[109] Let us point out only a few texts which come from different horizons within ancient Judaism, see *2 Baruch* 24.2; *Damascus Document* II.4; *M. Aboth*, V.2; *Targum of Isaiah* 42.14; *Sanhedrin* X.2.

[110] Cf. the parallels in L. Ginzberg, *The Legends of the Jews*, vol. V, p.174. The quotation from *1 Clement* is found in C. C. Richardson's *Early Christian Fathers*, New York, 1970, p. 47.

[111] Thackeray uses the formula with respect to the Septuagint which introduced the Scriptures to the non-Jewish world (in *The Septuagint and Jewish Worship*, London, 1921, p. 9). The formula is also correct in the sense that the Septuagint is the Old Testament that has "ripened" (as Barthélemy once said) and has become the Bible of the Christians. On the moral level, note the gloss of the targum for *Deuteronomy* 22.4 in regard to the prescription not to turn aside when one sees one's neighbor in difficulty (because his ox or ass has fallen). He must help him to lift the beasts and "dismiss (*šbq*) that which is in (his) heart against him". This is a good parallel to *Matthew* 5.23 or *Colossians* 3.13, which Billerbeck does not cite. Concerning the text itself see M. L. Klein, *The Fragment-Targums*, vol., I, p. 40; vol. II, p. 175. Compare the targums for *Exodus* 23.5 (*Onkelos, Neofiti* and *Ps-Jonathan*).

ly milieu of the successive generations of Jewish teachers. The targumic and homiletic traditions, on the contrary, born, developed, and transmitted in the liturgy of the synagogue, must have constituted a sort of average religious culture for all the Jews of that time. From what source was the piety of Joseph and Mary, John the Baptist and his parents nourished? Probably not only from the letter of the Old Testament. Certainly not from the learned discussions and quibbles of the sages. Their piety drew its life from a living tradition rooted in the Scriptures, inherited from post-exilic Judaism to which we owe perhaps the most inspiring texts of the Bible.[112]

Conclusions

This rapid sketch has made us penetrate into an intermediate world which was once called the "blank page between the Old Testament and the New" (David F. Strauss), into Christianity's infancy, before the umbilical cord between the Church and the Synagogue was severed (G. Ricciotti). Among the privileged witnesses to this important period (before Jews and Christians separated paths), are the translations of the Bible. These were heard by Christians and Jews in the same synagogues, during a period of time much longer than people usually think. It is unfortunate that research on the Judeo-Christians, that is, Christians who were intimately attached to Judaism by race, customs and traditions, has not yet produced definite results in spite of the brilliant works of J. Daniélou, E. Peterson, L. Goppelt, M. Simon, and H. J. Schoeps. These Christians who for a long time remained faithful to certain Jewish observances (circumcision, Sabbath, Easter celebrated on the 14th of Nisan) frequented the synagogues. Unfortunately sectarian deviations, anti-Jewish imperial policies, covert opposition

---

[112] Cf. G. F. Moore, *Judaism*, vol. I, p. 518, who writes, "That the common people had their religious conceptions directly from the Scriptures is unimaginable." D. Flusser has also highlighted the importance of Jewish religiosity in the intertestamental period for understanding the birth of the Christian religion: "A New Sensitivity in Judaism and the Christian Message", *HTR* 61 (1968) pp. 107-127.

of the Christians of Gentile origin, all aided in the eventual disappearance of the Jewish-Christians at about the beginning of the fifth century. They took with them many secrets concerning the history of the origins of the nascent Church.

Besides this advantage of bringing us back to the sources of Christianity, targumic studies are fruitful for various areas of research.

First of all, it is evident that the problem of the formation of the gospels can be understood along lines similar to the transmission of haggadic traditions, where, alongside a more or less uniform content, we find a formulation that varies from one manuscript to the other. One is always in the presence of changing forms within the same tradition. This is due to the very laws of oral tradition which J. Bédier, the well-known specialist of the *Chansons de geste*, summarized when speaking about a "very long series of songs... which have come down to us in three or four nearly contemporaneous redactions – continually dissimilar, yet continually identical."[113] One could compare the longer or shorter redactions of the Beatitudes or the Our Father in Matthew and Luke with the targum of *Exodus* 12.42 concerning the "Four nights" of salvation history where there is first a longer recension then another which seems to be a summary of the long one.

Even patristic studies could benefit from a better knowledge of the Jewish tradition. In particular, the Syrian fathers (Aphrahat, Ephrem) reveal a continuing relationship with Jewish writings. But Clement of Alexandria, Eusebius and Jerome also recognized and utilized this tradition.[114] If one could find the reasons for which Jerome translates *Isaiah* 16.1 "*Emitte Domine, Agnum dominatorem terrae....*" ("Send, Lord, the sovereign lamb of the earth"), one would no doubt see that it is not because of a distraction or because of a passing fantasy, for he seems to hold to it: "*Egredietur de te*

---

[113] *Histoire de la nation française*, vol. XII, p. 232 (cited by C. H. Dodd in *Mélanges A. Robert*, p. 404). On the connections between text and oral tradition see B. Gerhardsson, *Memory and Manuscript*, Uppsala, 1961; B. S. Childs, *Memory and Tradition in Israel*, London, 1962. Concerning the transmission of sacred texts see similar reflections offered by M. Black in *An Aramaic Approach*³, p. 280.

[114] Within this immense field one can find a preliminary orientation in E. Lamirande, "Etude bibliographique sur les Pères de l'Eglise et l'aggadah", *Vigiliae Christianae* 21 (1967) pp. 1-11.

Agnus immaculatus qui tollat peccata mundi, qui dominetur in orbe terrarum" ("From you will emerge the immaculate lamb who will take away the sins of the world, who will dominate the whole earth", PL 24, 171). This verse already has a messianic meaning in the targum which reads: "They shall bring tribute to the *Messiah* of Israel." The idea of sending a leader is explicit in one variant of Theodotion.[115] In any case, a number of objections against Jerome's interpretation do not at all take into account Jewish exegesis of the first century, which is most decisive when we are studying the possible use of similar passages in the New Testament.[116] This obscure Isaian passage could possibly be added to the well-known passages from the Apocryphal writings which proclaim the domination of the Lamb-Messiah, the prototype for the warrior Lamb of the Johannine apocalypse.[117] This is but one example which brings a larger problem to our attention.

Is it necessary to add that a better understanding of the variegated Jewish world of the first Century would help us to better appreciate the originality of "sectarian" doctrines such as those from Qumran, for which we have ample documentation, but which risk illuding us as to their exact position within Judaism in the first century?[118]

---

[115] See J. Ziegler, *Isaias*, Göttingen, 1939, p. 181, αποστειλατε (χαρ) αρχοντα. A. Jaubert has also indicated the interest of Jerome's version in *Approches de l'Evangile de Jean*, Paris, 1976, p. 138.

[116] See the commentary on Isaiah by J. Knabenbauer, F. Zorell in *Cursus scripturae sacrae...*, Paris, 1923, p. 381, "Messiam esse oriundum de Ruth nunquam dicitur" ("It was never said that the Messiah should be born from Ruth"). This objection would be valid if one were looking for the literal meaning of *Isaiah* 16.1, but not at all if one wishes to explain Jerome's exegesis. One could read an astonishing article by P. Lagrange, "Saint Jérôme et la tradition juive dans la Genèse", *RB* 7 (1893) pp. 563-566 where the author considers too exclusively the value of the translations of Jerome. On the connections between patristic literature and Jewish Tradition see L. Ginzberg, *Haggada bei den Kirchenvätern*, vol. I, Amsterdam, 1899; vol. II, Berlin, 1900; J. Daniélou, *Théologie du Judéo-Christianisme*, vol. I, Paris, 1958 (ET: *The Theology of Jewish Christianity*, London, 1964). Jewish legends still appear in the Christian literature of the Middle Ages and have exerted considerable influence on Christian art (cf. the columns and their famous capitals in the church of Vezelay in France [XII Century]).

[117] Cf. C. H. Dodd, *The Interpretation of the Fourth Gospel*, pp. 231-233.

[118] See R. Bloch, *RSR* 43 (1955) p. 197. M. R. Lehmann, "I Q Genesis

But the primary interest of the Aramaic versions is that they could be understood as a *praeparatio evangelica* ("preparing the way for the Gospel"). The best proof of their usefulness for understanding the content itself of the New Testament and Christian apologetics resides in the defiance and in the growing opposition of the Rabbis against this type of writing, leading to only one "authorized" recension, which conformed to official teaching, namely the Onkelos translation of the Torah and the recension of Jonathan ben Uzziel for the Prophets.[119]   Because of its many evidently edited passages, the *Codex Neofiti* may have had a quasi-official status (in the sense that it included commonly recognized traditions) in Palestine before it was superseded by the Babylonian targum (*Onkelos*).

Already the *Jerusalem Talmud* (*Berakhot V.3*) cites while criticizing the targumic commentary of *Leviticus* 22.28 mentioned above (around A.D. 350):

> They do not well those who interpret the attributes of the Holy One, blessed be He, as mercy, namely those who translate (*mtrgmnyn*): My people, the children of Israel! Just as I am merciful in heaven, so be you merciful upon earth. *Whether it be a cow or a ewe you shall not kill it with its young in one day.* They do not well as they interpret the decrees of the Holy One, blessed be He, as mercy.[120]

The Rabbinic writings also mention censored translations of *Exodus* 12.8; *Leviticus* 6.7; 18.21; *Deuteronomy* 14.5 and 26.4.[121] Most probably many haggadic sections were dropped because of their use by Christian authors. Ancient Rabbis such as Akiba and Tarfon (*Sanh.* 100b; *Shabbath* 116a), took positions against non-canonical books and against Apocryphal writings. Certain Rabbis even cast doubts on *Sirach* and *Qoheleth* "for they found in them

---

Apocryphon in the Light of the Targumim and Midrashim", in *Revue de Qumrân* 1 (1958) pp. 249-263.

[119] This reaction at the beginning of the second century explains the appearance of the Greek translation of Aquila (very literal) which was meant to replace the Septuagint which had been completely taken over by the Christians.

[120] On the problems which this text poses, see E. E. Urbach, *The Sages, Their Concepts and Beliefs,* Jerusalem, 1975, pp. 383-384. Compare McNamara, *The New Testament*, pp. 136-138.

[121] W. Bacher, *The Jewish Encyclopedia*, vol. XII, p. 58.

ideas that leaned towards heresy" (*Leviticus Rabbah*, 23.10).[122]
We know of the intervention by Rabban Gamaliel 1 (perhaps Paul's
teacher, according to *Acts* 22.3) in eliminating from circulation a
targum of *Job* by having it immured during a building operation on
the Temple mount (*Shabbat* 115a). All those who were given to
eschatological and messianic speculations found themselves excluded
from the next world (*Sanh.* X.1). At the end of the third century,
two Rabbis even wanted to forbid praying in Aramaic for the per-
emptory reason that "the Ministering Angels... do not understand
Aramaic" (*Shabbat* 12b). Since, in ancient days, prayer in Aramaic
was only associated with the study of the Law,[123] the caution expressed in regard to Aramaic paraphrases could have extended to the
language itself.

On the other hand, the Jews' distrust of the Septuagint is not
restricted to the authors of the Greek translations contemporaneous
with the beginnings of Christianity who replaced $\pi\alpha\rho\vartheta\acute{\epsilon}\nu\sigma\varsigma$ ("virgin") of *Isaiah* 7.14 with $\nu\epsilon\tilde{\alpha}\nu\iota\varsigma$ ("a young girl"; *cf. Exodus* 2.8).[124]
Thus R. Aron in *Les années obscures de Jésus* (Paris, 1960, p. 223)
also talks about "the Holy Book, watered down and falsified ever
since its first encounter with the Greek spirit."

*
*   *

In insisting on the importance of the Aramaic translations of
the Bible our purpose has not been to minimize the value and importance of other areas of research, particularly that being done on the
Dead Sea Scrolls. Attempting to explain everything through the
targums and ancient Jewish literature would be as ridiculous as
claiming to have found the core of the Christian message in the

---

[122] On this attitude of the Rabbis see J. Amussin, "Spuren antiqumrâni-
scher Polemik in der talmudischen Tradition", in *Qumrân-Probleme*, Berlin,
1963, pp. 5-27. D. S. Russell thinks that this concerned "the use of these
books in public recitation for liturgical or instructional purposes". (*The
Method and Message of Jewish Apocalyptic*, London, 1964, p. 33).

[123] D. Flusser, *Abraham unser Vater*, p. 141.

[124] Cf. D. Barthélemy, *Les devanciers d'Aquila*, Leiden, 1963, pp. 155,
203. Justin (*Dialogue* 71.2) reproaches the Rabbis for their attitude vis-à-vis
the Septuagint. See also W. D. Davies, *The Setting*, p. 282.

caves of the Judaean desert! But in the case of the targums, the continuity is more probable and recognizing the Aramaic Bible as one step toward Christianity means recognizing that Providence, by means of a living interpretation of Scripture, was making ready a "fulfillment" in Christ. Thus we can find there parallels which take nothing away from the originality of the New Testament, under the condition that we understand this originality as it should be understood.

The advantage of having recourse to ancient Jewish exegesis for understanding the origins of the Church is that it offers a sure starting point, the very text of the Old Testament, which should always be consulted first so as not to attribute to the commentator "discoveries" which in reality belong to the inspired text. Besides, this approach constitutes a possibility for an encounter between Jews and Christians. Study of the exegetical tradition places us in touch with the most profound and beautiful things that the Israelite soul has produced. Limiting the study of Judaism to the legal texts of the Talmud upon which we unfortunately project the invectives of the New Testament against the Pharisees, is both unjust and a false approach, just as unjust as thinking we could discover Christianity only by means of canon law and its commentators, or the works of the casuists. Within such a vast literature it is easy to discover weaknesses, to establish an anthology of them without realizing that these are the compilation of hundreds of authors whose opinions have been transcribed without any judgement of their value, and distributed over a time lapse of nearly ten centuries.[125]

When the Jews wish to present that which they hold to be the most precious in their religion, they draw from their haggadic traditions, and from their beautiful liturgical texts. Even the work entitled *Everyman's Talmud* (London, 1932) cites midrashim at least as often as it does the Talmud itself.[126]

---

[125] Read the admirable presentation of J. Goldin, "The Period of the Talmud", in L. Finkelstein (editor) *The Jews: Their History*, New York, 1970, pp. 119-224.

[126] By definition an anthology should collect the best examples. After so many malevolent "anthologies", we can but recommend that Christians be familiar with C. G. Montefiore - H. Loewe, *A Rabbinic Anthology*, New York, 1974. Even Bossuet (*Discours sur l'histoire universelle*, II, ch.21) recognized that "parmi une infinité de fables impertinentes... on trouve (dans le Talmud)

Is it superfluous to add that an encounter with this living and popular literature should lead to a more objective and also more sympathetic study of Jewish writings? Why speak about them as some French writers did, as *"fatras"*, *"broussailles"* or *"maquis"* (meaning "trash", "thickets", and "jungle"). If one of the principal paths, leading to a better comprehension of Christianity, obliges one to pass through those difficult roads, such judgments indeed will not encourage researchers to take them. Prejudices trap our minds and as habits of thought they are hard to break. It is true that in the last analysis a reciprocal secular ignorance must be corrected. We no longer live in an age when a medieval religious (Henry of Leiden) could introduce a citation by the formula *"Ut narrat rabbinus Talmud"* ("as Rabbi Talmud says").[127] Nor are we in 1541 when Francisco Machado talked about *Rabbi Midrash* in *The Mirror of the New Christians*; or in the XVII century, when a Spanish Fr. Labata believed that *Targum Yerushalmi* designated a certain Mr. Targum, a resident of Jerusalem, etc. We could easily make up a collection from pearls of this type.

Nevertheless it was possible to read recently, from the pen of an eminent exegete, the following enumeration of Aramaic paraphrases from the Bible: "The Targum Onkelos, Targum Jerushalmi I and II, Babylonian Targum", even though the last of these and Onkelos are in fact the same thing! But since targums are in vogue today, he thought it better to add one.

A change of attitude should also be seen in the manner in which this literature is used. Thanks be to God we are no longer interested in composing a *Pugio Fidei adversus Mauros et Judaeos*, a "dagger" meant "to chop off the head of the Jewish Holophernes", as was said by Pierre Chabelas, *doctor parisiensis* in his approval of the *editio princeps* of the famous book of Raymond Martini (Paris 1651). There is a need to study scientifically and objectively those documents bequeathed by ancient Judaism and to recover the lost features of its true image. At a talk given before a Christian audience, L. Ginzberg felt he had to pronounce the truism that it is

---

de beaux restes des anciennes traditions du peuple juif" (cited by J. Bonsirven, *Judaïsme palestinien*, vol. I, p. XIII).

[127] After all, the Russian peasants, Pierre Pascal told me once, believed also that the *Douma* was the wife of the tzar!

impossible to understand or interpret another religion without having a sympathetic attitude towards it.[128]

There is also here a way of allowing the true character of Christianity to appear: would not the Jews rejoice to see that we are defending the full worth of the Old Testament, which Tertullian (*Apologeticum* 19,2) calls "thesaurus... totius judaici sacramenti *et inde jam et nostri*" ("the treasure of the Jewish religion *and consequently ours as well*"); and wouldn't they also rejoice to see us recognize as a basic theological datum, that the New Testament is grafted on the Old as Israel had understood it, meditated it, lived and prayed it and that it is the same covenant which is, however, "new" (see *Romans* 11.29)? It would be salutary to return to this common root, before the mutual excommunications by which the image of both religious traditions was stamped by centuries of confrontation. Let us remember that the ministry of Christ was addressed only to Jews — the true Israel, and as such remaining the first to be called[129] — and that the Lord's prayer is a development of a Jewish prayer (the *Qaddish*).[130]

In short, Christians should have a clearer awareness of their Jewish roots and feel that they are "spiritually Semites", as Pope Pius XI once said.

In better recognizing the sources common to Judaism and Christianity, perhaps one day we will be able to hear a few dissonant notes at least resolve into an harmonious chord.

---

[128] "The Religion of the Jews at the Time of Jesus", *HUCA* 1 (1924) pp. 320-321.

[129] "The authentic expectation of Israel is still being prolonged". L. Bouyer, *La Bible et l'Evangile*, p. 251.

[130] Read the reactions of J. B. Frey in *RB* 12 (1915) pp. 556-563 concerning the monograph of D. de Sola Pool, *The Kaddish,* Leipzig, 1909, where the similarities are pointed out. At the end of the introduction of his *Corpus Inscriptionum Judaicarum* (vol. I, Rome, 1936, p. CXLIV) Frey cites the happy formula of Fr. Le Hir, the teacher of Ernest Renan: "Every time you encounter an idea common to the old and new people, be assured that the new people received this as a child from its mother, when still near its cradle".

Bibliography

Naturally this bibliography contains primarily works in the English language. I did not include all the works mentioned in the notes but only those which are of fundamental importance.

Alexander, P. S., *The Toponymy of the Targumim, with special reference to the Table of the Nations and the Boundaries of the Land of Israel*, D. Phil. Thesis, Oxford, 1974.

——, "The Targumim and Early Exegesis of 'Sons of God' in Genesis 6", *JJS* 23 (1972) pp. 60-71.

——, "The Rabbinic Lists of Forbidden Targumim", *JJS* 27 (1976) pp. 177-191.

Bacher, W., "Targum", *Jewish Encyclopedia* XII, pp. 57-63.

Bamberger, B. J., "Halakic Elements in the Neofiti Targum: A Preliminary Statement", *JQR* 66 (1975) pp. 27-38.

Bardtke, H., Editor, *Qumrân-Probleme*, Berlin, 1963.

Berliner, A., *Targum Onkelos*, Berlin, 1884.

Billerbeck, P. - H. L. Strack, *Kommentar zum neuen Testament aus Talmud und Midrasch*, 6 vols., Munich, 1922-1961.

Black, M., *An Aramaic Approach to the Gospels and Acts³*, Oxford, 1967.

——, "Aramaic Studies and the Language of Jesus", in *In Memoriam Paul Kahle* (eds. M. Black, G. Fohrer), Berlin, 1968, pp. 17-28.

Bloch, R., "Midrash", *DBS* V, cols. 1263-1281.

——, "Note méthodologique pour l'étude de la littérature rabbinique", *RSR* 43 (1955) pp. 194-227.

Bowker, J., *The Targums and Rabbinic Literature. An Introduction to Jewish Interpretations of Scripture*, Cambridge, 1969.

Brownlee, W. H., "The Habakkuk Midrash and the Targum of Jonathan", *JJS* 7 (1956) pp. 169-186.

Churgin, P., *Targum Jonathan to the Prophets*, New Haven, 1927.

——, *The Targum to Hagiographa*, New York, 1945 (in Hebrew).

Dalman, G., *Grammatik des jüdisch-palästinischen Aramäisch²*, Leipzig, 1905.

Díez Macho, A., *Neophyti I. Targum palestinense. Ms de la Biblioteca Vaticana*, 6 vols., Barcelona/Madrid 1968-1979 (English translation by M. McNamara and M. Maher).

Díez Macho, A., *Biblia Polyglotta Matritensia*, Series IV, *Targum palaestinense in Pentateuchum, Numeri*, Madrid, 1977; *Exodus, Leviticus, Deuteronomium*, Madrid, 1980.

——, "The Recently Discovered Palestinian Targum: its Antiquity and Relationship with the other Targums", *Supplements to Vetus Testamentum* 7 7 (1960) pp. 222-245.

——, *El Targum*, Barcelona, 1972 (Reprint Madrid, 1979).

——, "Le Targum palestinien", *Revue des Sciences religieuses* 47 (1973) pp. 169-231.

Ellis, E. E., "Midrash, Targum and New Testament Quotations", in *Neotestamentica et Semitica* (Festschrift M. Black), Edinburgh 1969, pp. 61-69.

Etheridge, J. W., *The Targums of Onkelos and Jonathan ben Uzziel on the Pentateuch with the Fragments of the Jerusalem Targum from the Chaldee*, 2 vols., London, 1862/1865 (Reprint New York, 1968).

Fitzmyer, J. A., *A Wandering Aramean. Collected Aramaic Essays*, Missoula, 1979.

Forestell, J. T., *Targumic Traditions and the New Testament* (SBL Aramaic Studies 4), Chico, Calif., 1979.

Geiger, A., *Urschrift und Übersetzungen der Bibel²*, Frankfurt am Main, 1928.

Ginzberg, L., *The Legends of the Jews*, 7 vols., Philadelphia, 1901-1938.

Ginsburger, M., *Das Fragmententhargum*, Berlin, 1899.

——, *Pseudo-Jonathan: Thargum Jonathan ben Usiël zum Pentateuch*, Berlin, 1903.

Grelot, P., "Les Targums du Pentateuque. Etude comparative d'après Genèse IV, 3-16", *Semitica* 9 (1959) pp. 59-88.

Grossfeld, B., *A Bibliography of Targum Literature*, 2 vols., New York, 1972/ 1977.

——, "Bible: Translations, Aramaic: the Targumim", *Enc. Judaica* IV, 1971, cols. 841-851.

——, *The Targum to the Five Megilloth*, New York, 1973 (Reprint of English translations).

——, M. Aberbach, *Targum Onkelos on Genesis 49* (Translation and Analytical Commentary), Missoula, 1976.

Hanson, A. T., *The New Testament Interpretation of Scripture*, London, 1980.

Harris, R., "Traces of Targumism in the New Testament", *Expository Times* 32 (1920-1921) pp. 373-376.

Heinemann, J., *Aggadah and its Development*, Jerusalem, 1974, (in Hebrew).

——, *Prayer in the Talmud. Forms and Patterns*, Berlin/New York, 1977.

——, "Remnants of Ancient *Piyyutim* in the Palestinian *Targum* Tradition", *Hasifrut* 4 (1973) pp. 362-375 (in Hebrew with an English summary).

——, "Early Halakhah in the Palestinian Targumim", *JJS* 25 (1974) pp. 114-122.

Jastrow, M., *A Dictionary of the Targumim, the Talmud Babli and Yerushalmi, and the Midrashic Literature*, New York/London 1886-1903 (Reprint New York, 1950).

Kahle, P., *Masoreten des Westens* II (Das palästinische Pentateuchtargum), Stuttgart, 1930.

——, *The Cairo Geniza*[2], Oxford, 1959.

Klein, M. L., *The Fragment-Targums of the Pentateuch According to their Extant Sources*, 2 vols. (Analecta Biblica 76), Rome, 1980 (Texts and translations).

Komlosh, Y., *The Bible in the Light of the Aramaic Translations*, Ramat-Gan, 1973 (in Hebrew).

Knudsen, E. E., *A Targumic Aramaic Reader*, Leiden, 1981.

Kutscher, E. Y., *Studies in Galilean Aramaic*, Ramat-Gan 1976 (=*Tarbiz* 21 <1950> pp. 192-205; 22 <1951> pp. 53-63, 185-192; 23 <1952> pp. 36-60).

Le Déaut, R., *La nuit pascale* (Analecta Biblica 22), Rome, 1963 (Second reprint 1980).

——, *Introduction à la littérature targumique*, Rome, 1966.

——, Robert, J., *Targum des Chroniques*, 2 vols., Rome, 1971 (Text and translation).

——, *Targum du Pentateuque*, 5 vols., (Sources chrétiennes), Paris, 1978-1981 (Translation only).

——, "The Current State of Targumic Studies", *Biblical Theology Bulletin* 4 (1974) pp. 3-32.

——, "Targumic Literature and New Testament Interpretation", *Biblical Theology Bulletin* 4 (1974) pp. 243-289.

——, "La tradition juive ancienne et l'exégèse chrétienne primitive", *Revue d'histoire et de philosophie religieuses* 51 (1971) pp. 31-50.

——, "Un phénomène spontané de l'herméneutique juive ancienne: le targumisme", *Biblica* 52 (1971) pp. 505-525.

Levey, S. H., *The Messiah: An Aramaic Interpretation. The Messianic Exegesis of the Targum*, New York, 1974.

——, "The Targum to Ezechiel", *HUCA* 46 (1975) pp. 139-158.

Levine, E., *The Aramaic Version of Ruth* (Analecta Biblica 58), Rome 1973 (Text and translation).

——, *The Aramaic Version of Jonah*, Jerusalem, 1975, (Text and translation).

——, *The Aramaic Version of Lamentations*, New York, 1976, (Text and translation).

——, *The Aramaic Version of Qohelet*, New York, 1978, (Text and translation).

Malina, B. J., *The Palestinian Manna Tradition. The Manna in the Palestinian Targums and its Relationship to the New Testament Writings*, Leiden, 1968.

McNamara, M., *The New Testament and the Palestinian Targum to the Pentateuch* (Analecta Biblica 27), Rome, 1966 (Second printing, with supplement containing additions and corrections, 1978).

——, *Targum and Testament. Aramaic Paraphrases of the Hebrew Bible: A Light on the New Testament*, Shannon/Grand Rapids, 1972.

——, "Targums", *Interpreter's Dictionary of the Bible*, Supp. Vol., Nashville, 1976, pp. 856-861.

——, "Jewish Liturgy and the New Testament", *The Bible Today*, n. 33 (1967) pp. 2324-2332.

Merx, A., *Chrestomathia targumica*, Berlin, 1888.

Miller, M. P., "Targum, Midrash and the Use of the Old Testament in the New Testament", *JSJ* 2 (1971) pp. 29-82.

Moore, G. F., *Judaism in the First Centuries of the Christian Era*, 3 vols., Cambridge, Mass., 1927-1930 (Reprint, 2 vols., New York, 1971).

Muñoz León, D., *Dios-Palabra. Memra en los Targumim del Pentateuco*, Granada, 1974.

——, *Gloria de la Shekiná en los Targumim del Pentateuco*, Madrid, 1977.

Newsletter for Targumic and Cognate Studies (1974 f.) (Department of Near Eastern Studies, University of Toronto, Ontario M5S-1A1).

Nickels, P., *Targum and New Testament. A Bibliography together with a New Testament Index*, Rome, 1967. (See Forestell).

Ploeg, J. P.M. van der, Woude, A. S. van der, *Le Targum de Job de la grotte XI de Qumrân*, Leiden, 1971.

Potin, J., *La fête juive de la Pentecôte*, Paris, 1971.

Rieder, D., *Pseudo-Jonathan. Targum Jonathan ben Uziel on the Pentateuch*, Jerusalem, 1974 (Text only).

Rodriguez Carmona, A., *Targum y Resurrección. Estudio de los textos del Targum palestinense sobre la resurrección*, Granada, 1978.

Shinan, A., *The Aggadah in the Aramaic Targums to the Pentateuch*, Jerusalem, 1979 (in Hebrew with English summary).

Sokoloff, M., *The Targum to Job from Qumran Cave XI*, Ramat-Gan, 1974.

Sperber, A., *The Bible in Aramaic*, Leiden, 1959-1973 (4 volumes of texts).

Stenning, J. F., *The Targum of Isaiah*, Oxford 1949 (Text and translation).

Stevenson, W. B., *Grammar of Palestinian Jewish Aramaic*[2], Oxford, 1962.

Vermes, G., *Scripture and Tradition in Judaism*[2], Leiden, 1973.

——, *Post-Biblical Jewish Studies*, Leiden, 1975.

——, "Bible and Midrash: Early Old Testament Exegesis", in *The Cambridge History of the Bible* I (1970) pp. 199-231.

——, in E. Schürer - G. Vermes - F. Millar, *The History of the Jewish People*, vol. I, Edinburgh, 1973, pp. 99-114 (with relevant bibliography).

Walton, B., *Biblia sacra polyglotta*, 6 vols., London, 1653-1657 (contains the targumic texts with Latin translations).

Wieder, N., "The Habakkuk Scroll and the Targum", *JJS* 4 (1953) pp. 14-18.

Wikgren, A., "The Targums and the New Testament", *Journal of Religion* 24 (1944) pp. 89-95.

York, A. D., "The Dating of Targumic Literature", *JSJ* 5 (1974) pp. 46-92.

——, "The Targum in the Synagogue and in the School", *JSJ* 10 (1979) pp. 74-86.

Zunz, L., *Die gottesdienstlichen Vorträge der Juden*², Frankfurt am Main, 1892 (Revised edition in Hebrew of Ch. Albeck, Jerusalem, 1950).

Indices

Old Testament

New Testament

Modern Authors